Personal Financial Planning: Cases & Applications Textbook

10TH EDITION 2017-2018

Financial Education

KAPLAN UNIVERSITY

SCHOOL OF PROFESSIONAL AND CONTINUING EDUCATION

At press time, this edition contains the most complete and accurate information currently available. Due to the nature of advanced designation examinations, however, information may have been added recently to the actual test that does not appear in this edition. Please contact the publisher to verify that you have the most current edition.

This publication is designed to provide accurate and authoritative information in regard to the subject matter covered. It is sold with the understanding that the publisher is not engaged in rendering legal, accounting, or other professional services. If legal advice or other expert assistance is required, the services of a competent professional should be sought.

PERSONAL FINANCIAL PLANNING: CASES & APPLICATIONS TEXTBOOK
10TH EDITION 2017-2018
©2017 Kaplan, Inc. All rights reserved.

Published by Kaplan Financial Education

Printed in the United States of America.

ISBN: 978-1-4754-6125-1

ADDITIONAL PRODUCTS AND SERVICES

Kaplan Financial Education Products

Personal Financial Planning Series:

- *Personal Financial Planning Theory and Practice, 9th Edition*
  Original authors: Michael A. Dalton, James F. Dalton, Scott A. Wasserman, Randall S. Guttery, and Randal R. Cangelosi

- *Understanding Your Financial Calculator, 6th Edition*
  Author: James F. Dalton

Kaplan Financial Education Review Courses for the CFP® Certification Examination Series:

- *Live and Web-Delivered Instructional Reviews*

- *Books 1–6: CFP® Exam Topics, Kaplan Financial Education Review for the CFP® Exam, July 2017 – March 2018 Exams*

- *Book 7: Case Book, Kaplan Financial Education Review for the CFP® Exam, July 2017 – March 2018 Exams*

- *Online Mock Exam and Solutions, Kaplan Financial Education Review for the CFP® Exam, July 2017 – March 2018 Exams*

- *Kaplan Financial Education Exam Prep Review Qbank for the CFP® Exam, July 2017 – March 2018 Exams*

- *Kaplan Financial Education Qbank for the CFP® Certification Examination, July 2017 – March 2018 Exams*

- *Kaplan Financial Education Core Lecture and Exam Tips Videos*

- *InstructorLink™ Ask an Instructor*

CFP Board-Registered Programs:

- Accelerated Certificate in Financial Planning:
  - Online Course
  - Traditional Classroom Program
  - Virtual Classroom Program
- University Programs Executive Certificate in Financial Planning
- Qualified Financial Advisor Online Program

For more information on any Kaplan Financial Education product, please call Customer Service at (877) 512-3290.

Contents

Foreword

INTRODUCTION

Personal Financial Planning Cases and Applications is primarily intended for use in the CFP Board-required Financial Plan Development Course, a case capstone course for a financial planning curriculum. It can also be used in a specific course such as Estate Planning as the questions in each case are identifiable by major topics (e.g., Insurance Planning, Investments, Estate Planning, etc.). This textbook includes 10 comprehensive financial planning cases. The cases are designed to help the student integrate the six major areas of personal financial planning:

- Fundamentals of Financial Planning
- Insurance Planning
- Investments
- Income Tax Planning
- Retirement Planning
- Estate Planning

CASES

Each case includes a complete family scenario that represents the information the financial planner has obtained from the client. Generally, each case scenario includes the following information:

- Personal background information
- Personal and financial goals
- Economic information
- Insurance information
- Investment information
- Income tax information
- Retirement information
- Gifts, estates, trusts, and will information

- Statement of cash flows

- Statement of financial position

- Information regarding assets and liabilities

- Additional exhibits

Note that the assumptions made in each case (e.g., interest rates) may or may not reflect the current economic environment. Assumptions should be used as given to master the applications of important financial planning topics.

The first four cases focus on all six topics of personal financial planning. The remaining six cases focus individually on the six major topics; however, they may be customized to cover additional areas through the use of the additional questions provided at the end of each case.

Case	Topic
Trenticosta	All
Morgan	All
Ross	All
Monroe	All
Redding	Fundamentals of Financial Planning
Clement	Insurance Planning
Peyton	Investments
Morrish	Income Tax Planning
Williams	Retirement Planning
Franklin	Estate Planning

EXHIBITS

Many of the cases have exhibits to add a sense of reality to the case. The exhibits include investment statements, wills, and trusts. The exhibits in each case provide the student with information within the textbook to answer many of the questions asked without having to refer to another textbook or source.

▌APPENDIX

The textbook contains an extensive appendix that should greatly assist the student in answering the questions and analyzing the cases. Exhibits on the following topics are included:

Major Financial Planning Area	Exhibit #	Brief Description of Selected Exhibits
Fundamentals	1–6	■ Financial planning process ■ Personal financial statements ■ Housing costs and debt repayment ■ Annual savings ■ Progress to retirement ■ Strengths and weaknesses
Insurance	7–12	■ Rating companies ■ Life insurance policy replacement ■ Homeowners policy summary ■ Covered perils ■ Eight general exclusions ■ Group Term Life Insurance—Cost of $1,000 protection
Investments	13–24	■ Total, systematic, and unsystematic risks ■ Risk pyramid ■ Area under the curve ■ Rates of return ■ Call and put options ■ Standard deviation ■ Performance measurements ■ Formulas
Income Tax	25-31	■ Tax rates and brackets ■ Standard deductions ■ Formula for individuals ■ Dependency exemption ■ Deductible travel expenses ■ Travel, entertainment, gift expenses, and reimbursements ■ Child and dependent care credit

Retirement	32-48	■ Retirement plans and comparisons
		■ ACP/ADP general rules (simplified)
		■ Section 79 costs for group term insurance
		■ Section 179 maximum writeoffs
		■ Comparison of defined benefit, defined contribution, and cash balance plans
		■ Indexed limits for pension and other plans
		■ Age-based profit-sharing illustration
		■ Fringe benefits by type
		■ Keogh worksheet for a tandem profit-sharing plan and money purchase pension plan
		■ IRA current phaseout limits for Traditional and Roth IRAs
		■ Annuities
		■ Indexed limits for pension and other plans
		■ Table III, uniform lifetime
		■ Self-employed person's rate table
		■ Summary of retirement plans
		■ Determining full retirement age
		■ Reduced retirement benefits for workers
Estates	49-58	■ Probate assets
		■ Unified tax rates and unified credit
		■ GSTT rates and exemptions
		■ Gift tax and estate formulas
		■ Trusts
		■ Reduction techniques and common mistakes
General	59-61	■ CFP Certification Examination Job Task Domains
		■ CFP Certification Examination Principal Topics
		■ Other Tax Limits

CHANGES FOR THE 10TH EDITION

Some questions from previous editions were deleted. This edition reflects changes brought about by recent tax updates and legislative changes, and are current as of printing.

The Case Method

The objective of the Personal Financial Planning Cases and Applications textbook is to prepare competent financial planners through the simulated practice of case analysis, identifying circumstances that should be addressed by financial planners, and making recommendations. Comprehensive questions serve as guides so students can accomplish these undertakings.

Personal financial planning case analysis is the process used to formulate financial recommendations for clients given the clients' current situation, expectations, and goals. Case analysis provides students with practice in bringing experience, theory, and common sense to bear in the formulation of plans and recommendations in realistic situations.

The case method class structure differs from the traditional lecture class structure in that the students must take a more active role in the learning process. The student must determine the problem, select the appropriate tools, and formulate a plan, all in the absence of full and complete information. Additionally, the student will be faced with the fact that often there is not one best plan of action. These complications are indicative of what a personal financial planner faces in the "real world."

While each student is unique and each case is different, students should develop a basic approach to analyzing cases. In reviewing the case scenario, the student will find it useful to briefly read the case scenario to get a feel for the clients and the overall case. Then, the student should reread the case in detail, making written notes to assure an in-depth comprehension of the case situation. The student may wish to subdivide the issues into the six major areas of personal financial planning:

- Fundamentals of Financial Planning

- Insurance Planning

- Investments

- Income Tax Planning

- Retirement Planning

- Estate Planning

The student should begin by identifying the strengths and weaknesses of the financial situation presented by the client in each area. It is important not to confuse symptoms with problems or to make premature evaluations. The student will often find that a problem in one area is related to and complicated by a problem in another area.

Once the student has a thorough understanding of the case situation and has begun to identify areas of concern, the student should then focus on answering the specific questions presented at the end of the case. With practice, the student should become more proficient in identifying the issues presented in the questions before reading the questions. A thorough understanding of the case information will help direct the student to both questions and answers.

Many of the questions direct the student to review the current or proposed situation and evaluate the appropriateness, effectiveness, soundness, or validity of such a situation. In the evaluation process, the student will need to understand the consequences of each decision and be able to suggest possible alternatives taking into consideration known and even unknown information. It is always important to keep in mind that it is the function of the personal financial planner to help clients optimize their situation in order to plan for both present and future needs, as well as their objectives.

The student should keep two important things in mind. The information presented here for each case is probably more complete and better organized than information which the client in practice presents to the professional financial planner. Furthermore, while ratios are intended to generate questions and to focus attention, they are not a perfect tool. By utilizing a variety of ratio measures, the student should get a good idea of debt management, savings rate, financial security, and progress towards financial security in retirement.

Acknowledgements and Special Thanks

We appreciate the tremendous support and encouragement we have received from everyone involved in the development of this project. We are extremely grateful to the users of our texts who provided us with valuable comments concerning all of our previous editions.

About the Authors

Michael A. Dalton, Ph.D., JD, CPA, CLU®, ChFC®, CFP®

- Former chair of the board of Dalton Publications, LLC.

- Associate professor of Accounting and Taxation at Loyola University in New Orleans, Louisiana (retired).

- Adjunct professor at George Mason University (2014 – present).

- Adjunct professor at Georgetown University (2001 – 2014).

- Former senior vice president, education at BISYS Group.

- Ph.D. in Accounting from Georgia State University.

- J.D. from Louisiana State University in Baton Rouge, Louisiana.

- MBA and BBA in Management and Accounting from Georgia State University.

- Former board member of the CFP Board's Board of Examiners, Board of Standards, and Board of Governors.

- Former member (and chair) of the CFP Board's Board of Examiners.

- Member of the Financial Planning Association®.

- Member of the *Journal of Financial Planning* Editorial Advisory Board.

- Member of the *Journal of Financial Planning* Editorial Review Board.

- Member of the LSU Law School Board of Trustees (2000 – 2006).

- Author of *Dalton Review for the CFP® Certification Examination: Volume I – Outlines and Study Guides, Volume II – Problems and Solutions, Volume III – Case Exam Book, Mock Exams A-1 and A-2 (1st – 8th Editions)*.

- Author of *Estate Planning (1st – 8th Editions)*.

- Author of *Retirement Planning and Employee Benefits (1st – 10th Editions)*.

- Author of *Fundamentals of Financial Planning (1st – 4th Editions)*.

- Author of *Insurance Planning (1st – 3rd Editions)*.

- Co-author of *Income Tax Planning for Financial Planners (1st – 7th Editions)*.

- Co-author of *Cases in Financial Planning: Analysis and Presentation (1st – 2nd Editions)*.

- Co-author of *Dalton CFA® Study Notes Volumes I and II (1st – 2nd Editions)*.

- Co-author of *Dalton's Personal Financial Planning Series – Personal Financial Planning Theory and Practice (1st – 3rd Editions)*.

- Co-author of *Dalton's Personal Financial Planning Series – Personal Financial Planning Cases and Applications (1st – 4th Editions)*.

- Co-author of *Cost Accounting: Traditions and Innovations* published by West Publishing Company.

- Co-author of the *ABCs of Managing Your Money* published by National Endowment for Financial Education.

James F. Dalton, MBA, MS, CPA/PFS, CFA®, CFP®

- Adjunct professor at George Mason University (2014 – present).

- Adjunct faculty member at Georgetown University (2002 – 2014).

- Former executive vice president, Assessment Technologies Institute, LLC.

- Former senior vice president, Kaplan Professional.

- Former president, Dalton Publications, LLC.

- Former senior manager of KPMG, LLP, concentrating in personal financial planning, investment planning, and litigation consulting.

- MBA from Loyola University, New Orleans.

- Master of Accounting in Taxation from the University of New Orleans.

- BS in Accounting from Florida State University in Tallahassee, Florida.

- Member of the CFP Board of Standards July 1996, Comprehensive CFP® Exam Pass Score Committee.

- Member of the AICPA and the Louisiana Society of CPAs.

- Member of the Financial Planning Association®.

- Member of the *Journal of Financial Planning* Editorial Review Board.

- Author of *Money Education's Quick Sheets*.

- Co-author of *Cases in Financial Planning: Analysis and Presentation (1st – 2nd Editions)*.

- Co-author of *Retirement Planning (1st – 10th Editions)*.

- Co-author of *Fundamentals of Financial Planning (1st – 4th Editions)*.

- Contributing author of *Insurance Planning (1st – 3rd Editions)*.

- Contributing author of *Estate Planning (1st – 8th Editions)*.

- Author of Kaplan Schweser's *Personal Financial Planning: Understanding Your Financial Calculator*.

- Author of Kaplan Schweser's *Understanding Your Financial Calculator for the CFA® Exam*.

- Co-author of *BISYS CFA® Study Notes Volumes I and II*.

- Co-author of Kaplan Schweser's *Personal Financial Planning: Cases and Applications*.

- Co-author of the *Kaplan Schweser Review for the CFP® Certification Examination, Volumes I – VIII* and Kaplan Schweser's *Financial Planning Flashcards*.

CONTRIBUTING AUTHORS

Kathy L. Berlin

- Senior Content Specialist, Kaplan Schweser.
- Successfully passed CFP® Certification Examination.
- Certified Public Accountant (Inactive).
- BA from Loyola University of New Orleans, Louisiana.
- Former CFO of a large nonprofit organization.
- Co-author of Kaplan Schweser's *Personal Financial Planning Cases and Applications, 5th – 10th Editions* textbooks and instructor guides.
- Co-author of Kaplan Financial's *Personal Financial Planning Theory and Practice, 4th – 9th Editions* textbooks and instructor guide.
- Co-author of the *Schweser Review for the CFP© Certification Examination, 9th – 18th Editions*.
- Co-author of the *Kaplan University/Kaplan Schweser Certification Examination Education Program, 4th – 14th Editions* materials.

Michael A. Harris

- Senior Content Specialist, Kaplan Financial Education.
- Successfully passed CFP® Certification Examination.
- Chartered Retirement Planning Counselor®.
- Accredited Asset Management Specialist®.
- Accredited Wealth Management Advisor®.
- Chartered Mutual Fund Counselor®.
- BS in Management from the United States Air Force Academy, Colorado Springs, Colorado.
- M.Div. from Southwestern Baptist Theological Seminary, Fort Worth, Texas.
- Served in the United States Air Force for seven years in OK, CA, ID, England, and NM.
- Former Senior Relationship Manager for a large nonprofit organization serving TX, OK, NM, AZ, AK, LA, IA, OH, KS, NE, MN, and WI.
- Over 25 years of experience in the insurance and securities business.

- Former General Securities Representative and life and health insurance agent.

- Co-author of Kaplan Schweser's *Personal Financial Planning Cases and Applications, 10th Edition* textbook and instructor guide.

- Co-author of Kaplan Financial's *Personal Financial Planning Theory and Practice, 10th Edition* textbook and instructor guide.

- Co-author of Kaplan University/Financial Education's *CFP® Exam Required Education Course Materials 2017.*

- Co-author of the *Schweser Review for the CFP® Certification Examination 2017 Exams.*

Jo Lynne Koehn, Ph.D., CPA, CFP®

- BKD Distinguished Professor of Accountancy at University of Central Missouri in Warrensburg, Missouri.

- Ph.D. in Accounting from University of Wisconsin, Madison.

- BS in Accounting and Management from Kansas State University in Manhattan, Kansas.

- Contributing author to *Personal Financial Planning Cases and Applications* textbook and instructor guide.

- Contributing author to *Financial Accounting Principles*, Wild and Shaw (Published by Irwin McGraw-Hill).

- Author of articles related to accounting and taxes in a variety of journals, including *The CPA Journal, Issues in Accounting Education, Journal of Theoretical Accounting Research, Strategic Finance, Taxes,* and *The Tax Adviser.*

Glen Kramer, MSF, CRPC®, CFP®

- Senior Content Specialist, Kaplan Schweser.

- BS in Economics from University of Wisconsin-Stevens Point.

- MSF from Kaplan University.

- Over 12 years of experience in the insurance and securities business.

- Former general securities representative.

- Former life and health insurance licensed sales representative in Arizona, Nevada, and Wisconsin.

- Co-author of Kaplan Schweser's *Personal Financial Planning: Cases and Applications, 9th and 10th Editions* textbooks and instructor guides.

- Co-author of Kaplan Financial's *Personal Financial Planning Theory and Practice, 8th and 9th Editions* textbooks and instructor guides.
- Co-author of the *Schweser Review for the CFP® Certification Examination, 15th – 18th Editions*.
- Co-author of the *Kaplan University/Kaplan Schweser Certification Examination Education Program, 8th – 14th Editions* materials.

Michael Long, CLU, ChFC, CFP®

- Senior Content Specialist, Kaplan Schweser.
- Over 25 years' experience in insurance and securities as a sales manager, classroom instructor, product manager, and advanced underwriting consultant.
- BS in business administration, Indiana State University.
- Co-author of Kaplan Schweser's *Personal Financial Planning Cases and Applications, 6th – 10th Editions* textbooks and instructor guides.
- Co-author of Kaplan Financial's *Personal Financial Planning Theory and Practice, 6th – 8th Editions* textbooks and instructor guides.
- Co-author of the *Schweser Review for the CFP® Certification Examination, 13th – 18th Editions*.
- Co-author of the *Kaplan University/Kaplan Schweser Certification Examination Education Program, 8th – 14th Editions* materials.

James Maher, CLU, ChFC, CFP®

- Senior Content Specialist, Kaplan Schweser.
- Former securities and insurance instructor, Kaplan Financial.
- Former insurance representative, General Securities.
- BBA from Florida International University.
- MBA from Kaplan University.
- Co-author of Kaplan Schweser's *Personal Financial Planning Cases and Applications, 6th – 10th Editions* textbooks and instructor guides.
- Co-author of Kaplan Financial's *Personal Financial Planning Theory and Practice, 5th – 9th Editions* textbooks and instructor guides.
- Co-author of the *Schweser Review for the CFP© Certification Examination, 12th – 18th Editions*.
- Co-author of the *Kaplan University/Kaplan Schweser Certification Examination Education Program, 6th – 14th Editions* materials.

Katheleen F. Oakley, MBA, CPA, CFP®*

- Currently serves as Academic Program Director for the Rice CFP® Certification Education programs and co-teaches the Case Analysis courses at Rice University.

- Co-author of *Cases in Financial Planning – Analysis and Presentation* textbook and instructor manual.

- Contributing author of *Personal Financial Planning: Cases and Applications* textbook and instructor guide.

- Consulting relationship with Houston Wealth Management Firm.

- Member of the CFP Board's Council on Education (2013 – 2015).

- Member of the Financial Planning Association.

- Member of the Texas Society of Certified Public Accountants, Houston Chapter.

- Former director of planning for Lincoln Financial Advisor's Southern Region, member of their National Planning team.

- Edited practice questions and answers contained in *Dalton CFA® Review, Volumes I and II Study Notes* and is a contributing author to the *Dalton CFA® Review Test Bank*.

- Former board member of the Pearland Economic Development Corporation.

- Former vice president and chief financial planning officer of Kanaly Trust Company.

- MBA and BS in finance from the University of New Orleans.

    * Licensed, not practicing.

Cindy R. Riecke, MSF, CLU, ChFC, CFP®

- Senior Director, Kaplan Schweser.

- BS in Business Administration from Louisiana State University in Baton Rouge, Louisiana.

- MSF from Kaplan University.

- Member of the Financial Planning Association.

- Former Director of Marketing Development for an international insurance and financial services company.

- Co-author of Kaplan Schweser's *Personal Financial Planning Cases and Applications, 5th – 10th Editions* textbooks and instructor guides.

- Co-author of Kaplan Financial's *Personal Financial Planning Theory and Practice*, *4th – 9th Editions* textbooks and instructor guides.

- Co-author of the *Schweser Review for the CFP© Certification Examination*, *9th – 18th Editions*.

- Co-author of the *Kaplan University/Kaplan Schweser Certification Examination Education Program, 4th – 14th Editions* materials.

Robert Showers, CPA, CFP®

- Associate Professor of Accounting—Emeritas at University of Central Missouri in Warrensburg, Missouri (1998 – 2013).

- Taught managerial accounting and personal finance at University of Central Missouri.

- Manages a private practice in Warrensburg, Missouri, offering investment and financial planning services to his clients.

- MBA from the University of South Dakota in Vermillion, South Dakota.

- BS from Morningside College in Sioux City, Iowa.

- Co-author of *Personal Financial Planning Cases and Applications* textbook and instructor guide.

Stephan E. Wolter, JD, MBA, ChFC

- Senior Content Specialist, Kaplan Schweser.

- Successfully passed July 2008 CFP® Certification Examination.

- JD from Indiana University, Indianapolis.

- MBA from University of Colorado at Colorado Springs.

- Co-author of Kaplan Schweser's *Personal Financial Planning Cases and Applications, 6th – 10th Editions* textbooks and instructor guides.

- Co-author of Kaplan Financial's *Personal Financial Planning Theory and Practice*, *6th and 9th Editions* textbooks and instructor guides.

- Co-author of the *Schweser Review for the CFP® Certification Examination, 13th – 18th Editions*.

- Co-author of the *Kaplan University/Kaplan Schweser Certification Examination Education Program, 7th – 14th Editions* materials.

Mary and Robert Trenticosta

Today is January 1, 2017. Mary and Robert Trenticosta have come to you, a financial planner, for help in developing a plan to accomplish their financial goals. From your initial meeting together, you have gathered the following information.

Personal Background and Information

Mary Trenticosta (Age 45)

Mary owns a closely held company, Crescent City Publications, Inc. She has been diagnosed with chronic back issues and is considering transferring some or all of her business interest to her son Dominic.

Robert Trenticosta (Age 24)

Robert is a nurse who works for an orthopedist in the building where Mary has her office.

The Trenticostas

Mary and Robert met when Mary sought treatment at the orthopedic clinic after she hurt her back. Mary and Robert have been married for two years.

The Children

Mary and Robert have no children together. Mary has two children from a former marriage: Valerie, age 18, who is a college student, and Dominic, age 27, who works in the publications business with Mary. The children's biological father is deceased.

Personal and Financial Objectives

1. Mary and Robert would like to retire at Mary's age 65 with a retirement income of $150,000 per year (in today's dollars). They would like you to calculate a retirement needs analysis to determine if they are on track to meet their goal.

2. Mary would like to begin ownership transfer of Crescent City Publications to her son, Dominic. She wants to begin by making a gift of 40% ownership and would like you to recommend the most efficient way to do so and explain the tax ramifications.

3. Mary is concerned about estate taxes and probate expenses and would like you to analyze their current situation and make recommendations for improvements.

4. Mary recently reviewed her equity brokerage account statement. She is happy with the recent positive returns of the stocks but is concerned about a market

correction. She definitely plans on holding the Small Company stock, but she would like you to evaluate the Big Company, Oil Company, and Auto Company stocks to determine if any of the holdings may currently be overvalued and ways to protect gains should the market decline.

5. Mary is considering liquidating some of her bond holdings because she believes interest rates are going to increase. Specifically, she wants to liquidate the bond mutual fund. She wants to know the income tax consequences of liquidating this fund.

Economic Information

■ They expect inflation to average 4% annually, both currently and for the long term.

■ They each expect salaries and net income to increase at 4% annually, both currently and long term.

■ They believe the S&P 500 is a good measure of the market's performance. The index has a historical annual rate of return of 12%, which they expect to continue.

Assumed Treasury Yield Curve

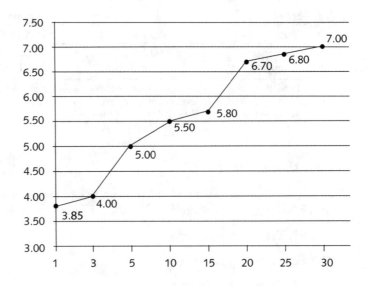

Economic Outlook—Investments

	Return	Standard Deviation
Small company stocks	13%	15%
Large company stocks	11%	12%
S&P 500 Index	12%	12%
Corporate bonds	8.5%	6%
Long-term treasury bonds	6.85%	5%
T-bills (90-day)	3.7%	2%

Insurance Information

Life Insurance

	Policy 1	Policy 2	Policy 3[1]
Insured	Mary Trenticosta	Mary Trenticosta	Robert Trenticosta
Face amount	$1,000,000	$300,000	$56,000
Policy type	Universal life	Term	Term
Cash surrender value	$10,000	$0	$0
Annual premium	$3,000	$300	$56
Beneficiary	Robert Trenticosta	Robert Trenticosta	Mary Trenticosta
Owner	Mary Trenticosta	Mary Trenticosta	Robert Trenticosta
Contingent beneficiary	Estate of Mary Trenticosta[2]	Estate of Mary Trenticosta[2]	Dominic and Valerie (equally)

[1]Robert's term policy is employer provided. The current year's premium has not been paid.
[2]Mary listed her estate as the contingent beneficiary because she was concerned about her husband's ability to pay off their debt obligations if she dies.

Health Insurance

Robert currently has a health insurance plan provided through his employer. Robert and Mary are both covered by his plan. Robert's plan has the following characteristics.

- $1,000 individual deductible

- $2,500 family deductible

- $4,000 stop-loss limit

- 80/20 coinsurance

Note: Valerie is also covered under this plan as a dependent.

Crescent City Publications does not have a health insurance plan. Dominic is currently covered under his wife's health insurance policy.

Disability Insurance

Robert has disability coverage through his employer (60% of gross salary, own occupation, 90-day elimination period). Crescent City Publications does not provide disability insurance to its employees. Mary has purchased an individual disability policy. The policy has an own occupation definition of disability and provides 65% of gross salary after a 180-day elimination period. The premium is $2,400 per year, and the policy provides benefits to age 65.

Property and Liability Auto Insurance

	Mary and Robert's Cars	Valerie's Car
Policy type	Personal auto policy	Personal auto policy
Liability (bodily injury)	$250,000/$500,000	$100,000/$300,000
Property damage	$100,000	$50,000
Medical payments	$2,000	$2,000
Physical damage, own car	Actual Cash Value	Actual cash value
Uninsured motorist	$250,000/$500,000	N/A
Collision deductible	$1,000	N/A
Comprehensive deductible	$1,000	N/A
Annual premium	$3,600 (two cars)	$2,700

Homeowners Insurance

	Personal Residence	Ski Condo
Policy type	HO-3	HO-6
Dwelling	$300,000	$0*
Other structures	$30,000	$0
Personal property	$150,000	$150,000
Personal liability	$200,000	$200,000
Medical payments	$2,000	$2,000
Deductible	$500	$1,000
Coinsurance requirement	80%	80%
Annual premium	$3,000	$2,200
*1,000 on owner's additions and alterations		

Personal Liability Umbrella Insurance

The policy coverage is for $4 million, and the premium is $600 per year.

Investment Information

The Trenticostas have a required rate of return of 9%. They consider themselves to be moderate to moderate-aggressive investors, and they consider $100,000 an adequate amount for an emergency fund.

Income Tax Information

In 2016, the Trenticostas are in the 28% marginal federal income tax bracket and capital gains are taxed at 15%. There is no state income tax.

Retirement Information

Robert is eligible to participate in his employer's Section 401(k) plan, but he has chosen not to participate. His employer provides a dollar-for-dollar match of up to 3% of his gross salary. No contributions have been made to the account on Robert's behalf by the employer.

Mary does not have a retirement plan at Crescent City Publications, but she usually makes individual retirement account (IRA) contributions for Robert and herself. Mary has several other retirement accounts from previous employers, all of which are qualified plan assets.

Mary and Robert would both like to retire when Mary reaches age 65. They believe that together they would need about $150,000 (in today's dollars) annual pre-tax income during their retirement.

They both expect to live to age 95.

Gifts, Estates, Trusts, and Will Information

Gifts

Neither Mary nor Robert has made any previous taxable gifts.

Estates

Mary and Robert estimate that funeral expenses will be $50,000 and administrative expenses will be $80,000 each.

Wills

Mary has a will that leaves $1 million to each child with the remainder of the estate going to the surviving spouse. Robert has a will that leaves everything to Mary. Mary is interested in other estate planning techniques that would maximize the actual transfer to the children but still protect Robert for his life.

STATEMENT OF CASH FLOWS
Mary and Robert Trenticosta
Expected For the Year 2017

CASH INFLOWS

Salary—Mary	$120,000	
Salary—Robert	56,000	
Investment income	31,417	
Rental income	4,200	
TOTAL CASH INFLOWS		$211,617

CASH OUTFLOWS

Ordinary living expenses

Savings—IRA contributions	$ 10,000	
Savings—bond mutual fund income reinvestment	12,000	
Food	9,600	
Clothing	5,000	
Travel	7,000	
Entertainment at home	3,000	
Utilities	6,000	
Telephone	7,200	
Auto maintenance	4,800	
Pool service	1,400	
Lawn service	1,680	
Church	2,400	
Total ordinary living expenses		$70,080

Other payments

Automobile payment	$ 14,400	
Mortgage payment (principal residence)	23,494	
Mortgage payment (ski condo)	25,886	
Total other payments		$63,780

Insurance premiums

Automobile	$ 6,300	
Disability	2,400	
Homeowners	5,200	
Life	3,300	
Umbrella	600	
Total insurance premiums		$ 17,800

(Continued on next page)

insurance refers to liabilities insurance that is in excess of specified other policies & also potent. primary insurance for losses not covered by the other policies.

STATEMENT OF CASH FLOWS
Mary and Robert Trenticosta
Expected For the Year 2017 *(continued)*

Taxes

Federal income tax	$31,702	
FICA—Robert ($56,000 × 7.65%)	4,284	
FICA—Mary ($120,000 × 1.45% + $118,500 × 6.2%)	9,087	
Property tax (principal residence)	1,000	
Property tax (ski condo)	600	
Total taxes		$ 46,673
TOTAL EXPENSES AND PLANNED SAVINGS		$ 198,333
NET CASH FLOW (SURPLUS)		$ 13,284

Notes:

Investment income:		
	Checking	$ 0
	Savings	1,528
	Money market account	401**
	Equity brokerage account	3,188
	Bond mutual fund	12,000*
	Bond portfolio	12,500
	High-Tech Stock	1,600
	Brown Foreman Stock	200
	TOTAL	$31,417

*All income is automatically reinvested in the bond mutual fund.
**Current interest paid on money market account is 2%.

STATEMENT OF FINANCIAL POSITION
Mary and Robert Trenticosta
As of January 1, 2017

	Assets[1]				Liabilities[2,3] and Net Worth	
	Cash and cash equivalents				**Liabilities**	
JT	Checking[4]	$	16,000	S1	Automobile notes payable	$ 38,000
S2	Checking[5]		10,000	S2	Credit cards	7,000
JT	Savings[6,7]		50,950	JT	Mortgage on residence	$ 278,300
	Total cash and equivalents	$	76,950	S1	Mortgage on ski condo	215,254
	Invested assets				**Total liabilities**	**$ 538,554**
S1	Stock in Crescent City Publications[8]	$	320,000		**Net worth**	**$ 2,941,334**
S1	Equity brokerage account		116,242			
S1	Bond mutual fund		272,000			
S1	Bond brokerage account		200,000			
S1	High-Tech Stock[9]		40,000			
S2	Brown Foreman Stock[10]		10,000			
S1	Pension plan #1[11]		569,188			
S1	Pension plan #2[11]		697,352			
S1	IRA rollover[11]		130,156			
S1	IRA		29,300			
S2	IRA		34,700			
S1	Cash surrender value life insurance		10,000			
	Total invested assets	$	2,428,938			
	Use assets					
JT	Personal residence[6]	$	360,000			
S1	Ski condo		240,000			
JT	Personal property[6]		200,000			
S1	Automobiles (3)		174,000			
	Total use assets	$	974,000			
	Total assets	**$3,479,888**		**Total liabilities and net worth**		**$3,479,888**

Notes
[1] Assets are stated at fair market value with exception of Crescent City Publications stock.
[2] Liabilities are stated at principal only.
[3] All liabilities go with the associated asset for title purposes.
[4] This is joint tenancy with right of survivorship with son, Dominic. Checking account does not earn interest. Mary contributed 100%.
[5] Robert has a POD on the checking account naming Mary as the beneficiary.
[6] Joint tenancy with right of survivorship with spouse.
[7] The current interest rate for savings accounts is 3%.
[8] This is Mary's guess for the FMV of Crescent City Publications. Her basis is $50,000.
[9] 2,000 shares at $20 per share. The current dividend is $0.80 per share and is expected to grow at 3% per year.
[10] 200 shares.
[11] All pension plans have the spouse of participant as the named beneficiary.

Title Designations
S1 = Mary (sole owner)
S2 = Robert (sole owner)
JT = Joint tenancy with right of survivorship

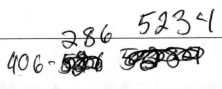

Information Regarding Assets and Liabilities

High-Tech Stock

Mary's brother, Brian, gifted this stock to Mary as a Christmas present after purchasing it on October 15, 2012. Brian's basis in the stock was $17,000, and the value at the date of the gift was $50,000. The current value of the stock is $40,000. The stock currently pays an annual dividend of $0.80. See Footnote 9 on the Statement of Financial Position.

Bond Mutual Fund

Mary inherited the bond mutual fund from her uncle, Gary, who died December 10, 2014, at which time the fund was valued at $296,000. Gary had just bought the fund on November 1, 2014, and invested $290,000. All earnings are automatically reinvested in the fund, and Mary has had no distributions since inheriting it. The fund has reinvested income of $12,000 in 2016, but unfortunately is only valued at $272,000 today due to changes in interest rates.

Bond Brokerage Account

Description	Maturity (Years)	Coupon[1]	Duration	Cost Basis	Fair Market Value
20,000 U.S. T-bills	1	N/A	1.00	$ 19,280.00	$ 19,286.40
40,000 U.S. T-bonds	30	8%	13.00	40,000.00	44,988.94
20,000 U.S. T-bonds	20	0%	20.00	2,626.00	5,250.60
40,000 Big Company bonds[2]	20	9%	10.81	40,000.00	48,542.02
30,000 Weak Company bonds[3]	25	9%	3.23	30,000.00	6,000.94
50,000 Texas municipal bonds	15	6%	10.54	50,000.00	55,232.58
				$181,906.00	$179,301.48
Money market account					$ 20,698.52
TOTAL (1/1/17)					$200,000.00

Notes
[1] Assume all coupon payments are made once a year.
[2] Bonds are investment quality.
[3] Bonds are non investment quality.

Equity Brokerage Account

Stock[1]	Shares	Beta	Standard Deviation	Dividend Yield[2]	Average Return	Cost Basis	Fair Market Value
Big Company	2,000	0.88	12.5%	4.0%[3]	12.5%	$16,092.94	$ 29,000.00
Small Company	2,000	1.24	18.0%	0.0%	15.0%	21,448.70	24,666.00
Oil Company	2,000	1.00	10.0%	3.5%[3]	8.0%	22,271.40	30,300.00
Auto Company	2,000	1.12	10.0%	3.0%[4]	10.0%	24,249.44	32,276.00
					Total	$84,062.48	$116,242.00

Notes

[1] The stock portfolio has a correlation coefficient with the market of 0.80.

[2] The dividend yield is the current yield.

[3] The growth of the dividend is expected to remain at 3%.

[4] The expected growth of the dividend is zero.

Brown Foreman Stock

Robert inherited the stock from his great-aunt Sarah who died in 2015 and who had bought the stock when the price was $42 per share. When Sarah died, she left Robert 100 shares of Brown Foreman stock. Robert knows that on the date of Sarah's death the stock closed at $35 per share with a high price of $38 and low price of $34. The stock has since split two-for-one and has a current dividend yield of 2%. Sarah's executor did not elect the alternate valuation date.

Personal Residence

The Trenticostas purchased their personal residence for $350,000 nine months ago. They put down 20% from the sale of their previous home. They were able to get a mortgage rate of 7.5% financed over 30 years. Their monthly payment is $1,957.80 (P & I) with a balance of $278,300.78 and 352 payments remaining.

Ski Condo

Mary purchased the ski condo three years ago for $300,000 and put 20% down. The balance was financed over 15 years at 7%. The monthly payment is $2,157.18 (P & I), and they have made 30 payments. The outstanding balance is $215,254.14. Since the purchase of the condo, Mary has incurred the following restoration costs.

Wood floors	$4,000
Furniture	7,000
Ceiling fans	600
Carpet	2,400
Kitchen appliances	4,400
Total	$18,400

The Trenticostas use the condo quite often in the winter and summer, but they are usually able to rent it to friends for 14 days per year at $300 per day.

QUESTIONS

1. List the Trenticostas' financial strengths and weaknesses.

2. After reading the case, what additional information would you request from the Trenticostas to complete your data-gathering phase?

3. If Mary were to die today, what would be the value of her probate assets?

4. Evaluate Mary's current estate plan.

5. What would be the value of Robert's probate assets if he died today?

6. Mary is considering liquidating the bond mutual fund and expects to receive net proceeds of $272,000 from the sale. What are the tax consequences of such a sale, assuming that it takes place on April 15, 2017?

7. Mary is considering disposing of her stock in Crescent City Publications by one or more of the following methods: grantor retained annuity trust (GRAT), private annuity, charitable remainder annuity trust (CRAT), or self-canceling installment note (SCIN). Which method or methods are reasonable under the circumstances? Any sale contemplates getting the value of the stock out of her gross estate.

8. Which of Mary's assets would be the best choice to gift to her children if the objective is estate minimization?

9. Mary is considering making a gift of 40% of Crescent City Publications to her son, Dominic. She discussed this transaction with a valuation expert who told her the company is probably worth $350,000. The valuation expert also says that with the transfer of the 40% share she could apply a valuation discount of 50%. Answer the following questions, assuming that Mary makes the gift with the above appraisal information.
   a. What is the value of the total gift?
   b. What are the requirements if Mary and Robert decide to make the split-gift election?

10. If Mary and Robert can earn their required rate of return, how much would they need when Mary is age 65 to provide for both of them in retirement? (Round to the nearest thousand and assume they are both expected to live to age 95.)

11. Which bonds in the bond portfolio are subject to:
    a. Default risk?
    b. Reinvestment rate risk?
    c. Exchange rate risk?
    d. Interest rate risk?
    e. Liquidity risk?

12. How would Mary protect her gain in Big Company stock without selling the stock?

13. Determine the yield to maturity for each bond using the current fair market value.

14. Excluding the money market funds, what is the duration of the bond portfolio in the bond brokerage account?

15. How have interest rates changed during the holding period of the bonds in the brokerage account?

16. The Trenticostas have how much in cash and cash equivalents?

17. Using the capital asset pricing model, determine the expected return for each of the stocks in the portfolio.

18. Determine Jensen's alpha for each of the stocks in the brokerage account. Assume that the actual returns are as follows:

	Actual Return
Big Company	13.0%
Small Company	13.5%
Oil Company	9.0%
Auto Company	10.5%

19. What is the expected return of the stock portfolio in terms of dollars? In percentage terms?

20. You are meeting with the Trenticostas to develop a retirement planning strategy. During the meeting, you have proposed a number of strategies that will help the couple reach their goals. The couple has agreed with you to transfer some of their existing assets to a portfolio of mutual funds based on a specific allocation. What should you do next?

21. Assuming an income tax rate of 28%, what is the after-tax equivalent yield to maturity for the Texas municipal bonds?

22. On the basis of other prevailing interest rates, does the pretax return for the Texas municipal bond seem reasonable? Why?

23. Determine the holding period return for each of the stocks in the equity brokerage account. Ignore dividends for this purpose.

24. What percentage of the change in the value of the equity brokerage account can be explained by changes in the stock market?

25. On the basis of the constant growth dividend discount model, what must the Trenticostas' required rate of return be for the High-Tech stock to be priced fairly? What are the implications of buying, selling, or holding the stock?

26. Mary only recently made Dominic the joint tenant of her checking account. What are the consequences to Mary? When does this become a taxable gift from Mary to Dominic?

27. Determine Robert's basis in the Brown Foreman stock.

28. If Robert were to sell the Brown Foreman stock today, what would be the income tax consequences?

29. How much qualified residence interest may the Trenticostas deduct for income tax purposes in 2017?

30. By using the constant growth dividend discount model, determine the value per share for each of the following stocks.

    a. Big Company
    b. Oil Company
    c. Auto Company

31. Since Mary was diagnosed with chronic back issues, she has been distracted by her health concerns and forgot to make her IRA contribution for 2016. Can she still make a 2016 contribution in 2017?

32. Mary wants your help in determining the probability of achieving certain returns within her portfolio.

    a. Determine the probability of getting a positive return for the Big Company.
    b. Determine the probability of getting a return above 30% from Auto Company.
    c. Determine the probability of earning a return between 15% and 33% for Small Company.

33. Mary is considering rebalancing her equity brokerage account portfolio by selling the Oil Company stock and the Auto Company stock. She wants to invest the entire portfolio as follows:

    ■ 60% in Small Company
    ■ 40% in Big Company

    The two stocks have a tendency to not move together because the correlation between them is only 0.3. If Mary sells the stock today at the current FMV and pays 15% capital gains tax out of this portfolio, how much will be invested in the Big Company and Small Company?

34. What is the expected return for this new portfolio? Assume the same facts as in the previous question.

35. What will be the standard deviation of her new portfolio? Use the same facts as in the previous questions.

36. Mary and Robert have the following income and expenses from the rental of the condo during 2016.

Rental Income (14 days at $300 per day)	$4,200
Interest Expense	$14,714
Property Tax	$600
Depreciation	$9,600
Utilities	$2,000

    How should they treat the above items on their 2016 federal income tax return?

37. Mary has outpatient surgery in January 2017 to remove a small growth from her arm. She incurs $3,200 in expenses. How much will she have to pay (i.e., how much is not covered by the health insurance policy)?

38. Crescent City Publications had earnings of $54,000 last year. How does the capitalized earnings approach method of valuation compare with Mary's guess of what Crescent City is worth? Use the Trenticostas' required rate of return.

39. Based on the earnings of $54,000, how does Mary's guess of the value of Crescent City compare with using the P/E ratio of similar companies to determine the value of Crescent City? Assume the P/E ratio for similar companies is 12.

40. If Mary sold the ski condo and all the contents in 2017 for $320,000, how much tax would she pay from this sale? Assume a real estate commission of 6%.

Use the following information for questions 41 through 45.

Mary is concerned about the price of Big Company falling in the near future. During July 2017, she decides to buy put options to protect her position in the stock. The price of the stock has dropped to $14 per share. The options have an expiration date of January 2018, an exercise price of $13, and a premium of $2 per contract.

41. How many option contracts should she buy to fully hedge her long position in Big Company stock?

42. Mary fully hedges her position with the above option. On December 31, 2017, the price of the stock has dropped $10.
    a. What is her total unrealized gain or loss on the option contracts?
    b. How much gain or loss does she have to recognize on her 2017 Form 1040?
    c. How much is the gain or loss on her long position in Big Company for the time she has held these option contracts?
    d. Based on your analysis, has Mary done an effective job of hedging Big Company stock? If not, why? What alternative strategy might you suggest? Describe the pros and cons of the put option strategy and your suggestions, if applicable.

43. In January 2018, the option expires unexercised. The price of Big Company has increased to $15 per share. How should Mary treat this on her 2018 individual tax return (Form 1040)?

44. Because the price of Big Company stock has rebounded and the entire market is doing well, Mary believes that the price of Big Company will continue to increase above the $14.50 level (current price). How do you advise her as her financial planner?

45. After your discussion with her, Mary decides to enter into a futures contract on the S&P 500 to take advantage of the rising market. The contract expires January 2019.
    a. Should she buy or sell the contract?
    b. The S&P 500 contract has had the following prices:

Upon entering into contract	$100
At 12/31/17	$110
Expiration	$125

    How much gain or loss should Mary report for tax purposes in 2017 and 2018? What is the nature of this gain or loss?

46. If Mary and Robert died, how should their beneficiaries treat the inherited IRAs?

47. The Trenticostas are concerned about future estate taxes. Mary has been reading about strategies to reduce estate taxes and learns the proceeds of her life insurance will be received tax free by the beneficiary but will be included in her estate because she is the owner of the policies. She plans on leaving $1 million each to her children, Valerie and Dominic. She determines she can accomplish two goals at once and changes the beneficiary of her $1 million life insurance policy to her daughter, Valerie, and makes Robert the owner of the policy to remove the proceeds from her gross estate. What are the tax consequences of Mary's idea?

48. While working in the orthopedic office, Robert slips and falls, severely fracturing his arm. The fracture requires surgery and a cast, as well as several weeks of rehabilitation. Robert is unable to perform his nursing duties for four months, but he does try to help out at the office whenever possible. Robert receives a $5,000 workers' compensation payment for medical expenses, as well as any benefits due from his disability insurance coverage. Additionally, for the hours Robert helped out at the office over the four month period, Robert was paid a total of $5,000. Assuming Robert is in a 28% marginal tax bracket, how much money, after taxes, has he received over the four month period?

49. Mary is pleased that Valerie is attending college and studying business, as she hopes Valerie will become interested in one day working at Crescent City Publications. In 2017, as a reward and incentive to stay in college, Mary gives Valerie her brokerage account to help pay for college, and, hopefully, graduate school. As the brokerage account was Mary's prior to meeting Robert, she did not consult Robert in the education funding arrangement. Assuming the equity brokerage account continues its current yield and that all of the stocks produce dividends, what are the tax consequences of this education funding plan?

50. Mary's will bequeaths $1 million each to Valerie and Dominic. Mary worries that leaving $1 million in a lump sum will lead to money management problems and mistakes for Valerie and Dominic, as neither is a savvy investor. She has decided to amend her will and create a testamentary trust, into which $2 million of her assets will be placed. The trust assets will be professionally managed with a distribution schedule of the assets to Valerie and Dominic over a period of years. Calculate Mary's probate estate to reflect the testamentary trust.

51. Assume at the time of Mary's death Pension Plan #1, Pension Plan #2, and the ski condo have each grown in value to a FMV of $1 million. What would be the tax consequences if Robert immediately liquidated Pension Plan #1 and the ski condo for the date of death FMV to obtain the capital needed to start his own business?

52. On November 10, 2017, Mary purchased stock with a FMV of $50,000 in her equity brokerage account. On December 12, 2019, when the stock has a FMV of $40,000, Mary gifts the stock to Valerie. What would be Valerie's basis, holding period, and gain or loss if she then sold the securities one month later for:
    a. $38,000
    b. $55,000
    c. $45,000

53. Assume Mary made a gift of property in 2016 with a fair market value of $100,000 and an adjusted basis of $40,000 to Dominic. What would Dominic's basis in the property be if Mary paid gift taxes of $20,440 (assume that at time of this gift, she has previously used all of her lifetime exemption amount) and applied an annual exclusion to the transfer.

54. Assume Big Company stock is currently paying a dividend of $.58 per share. Rather than the dividend growing at a steady 3%, assume the dividend is expected to grow for three years at 6% and then 7% annually thereafter. Furthermore, assume that the Trenticostas' required rate of return is 9%. What is the intrinsic value of Big Company based on the multistage growth dividend discount model?

55. Assume that Mary first raises the idea of disposing of her Crescent City Publications stock after you have entered into your planning relationship with the Trenticostas. You quickly realize the techniques she mentions for accomplishing the transfer (GRATs, private annuities, CRATs, and SCINs) are beyond your expertise as a planner. What are your ethical obligations to the Trenticostas?

56. Assume that shortly after your meeting with the Trenticostas, Valerie calls you and tells you she is concerned because Dominic has told her he will inherit Crescent City Publications from their mother. Valerie feels this would be unfair and asks you to confirm whether it is true. She also asks you whether her mother has made any financial provisions for her. What ethical concerns does Valerie's call present to you, and how might you address them?

57. You feel a clearer picture of the Trenticostas' financial position can be rendered by classifying liabilities on the Statement of Financial Position as current liabilities and long-term liabilities. What is your next step in creating this statement?

2

Peter and Patricia Morgan

Today is January 1, 2017. Peter and Patricia Morgan have come to you, a financial planner, for help in developing a plan to accomplish their financial goals. From your initial meeting together, you have gathered the following information.

Personal Background and Information

Peter Morgan (Age 62)

Peter has been employed 25 years as a vice president for an oil field services company. He participates in a defined benefit plan. Peter's first wife is deceased.

Patricia Morgan (Age 29)

Patricia owns two companies: Publications, Inc., and Patricia Advertising, Inc.

The Morgans

Peter and Patricia met in July 2011 and were married in November of the same year. They have no children together.

Peter's Children

Peter has four children from his first marriage.

Martin	Age 34
Julius	Age 33
Brad	Age 32
Laena	Age 31

All of the children are healthy, employed, married, and none are living with Peter and Patricia. Peter has several grandchildren.

Patricia's Family

Patricia's parents are deceased but before her marriage to Peter she had been living with her grandmother, Natalie Fortune, a recent widow, who is 81 years old. Patricia's grandfather, Robert, died November 19, 2016, after a long illness during which Patricia helped with his care. Natalie and Patricia are the only beneficiaries of Robert's will. Natalie is in good health for her age but no longer drives and has been relying on Patricia for transportation for shopping, doctor's appointments, and visiting friends. Because Peter and Patricia want to travel now that he is retiring, Patricia and Natalie are looking for alternatives so Natalie's lifestyle is not negatively impacted by the Morgans' plans. Natalie lives in the same home she has lived in for 50 years. Robert's estate is still in probate.

Personal and Financial Objectives

1. Patricia has agreed to sell Publications, Inc., for $900,000 on April 1, 2017, to a business syndicate. The terms are 20% down on April 1, and the balance paid in equal monthly installments over 10 years at 11% interest beginning May 1, 2017. The Morgans have asked you to explain the tax implications of the installment sale for the 2017 tax year.

2. Patricia would also like you to analyze the tax implications if she sells Patricia Advertising, Inc., for its current fair market value.

3. Peter is retiring and wants your help in analyzing the options available to him from his employer's defined benefit pension plan. He is uncertain as to which option to select. Peter's life expectancy is 25.75 years. Patricia's life expectancy is 57.75 years, which is also their joint life expectancy.

4. The Morgans would like you to review their various insurance plans and offer feedback.

Economic Information

- They expect inflation to average 3% (consumer price index) annually over both the short and long term.

- They expect returns of 11% annually on the S&P 500 Index.

- 90-day T-bills are currently yielding 2%.

- Current mortgage rates are 4.25% for a fixed 15-year mortgage and 6% for a fixed 30-year mortgage.

- Mortgage closing costs are expected to be 3% of any mortgage.

Insurance Information

Life Insurance

	Policy 1	Policy 2
Insured	Peter	Patricia
Owner	Peter	Patricia
Beneficiary	Children	Peter
Face amount	$450,000	$450,000
Cash value	$0	$0
Policy type	Term	Term
Settlement option	Lump sum	Lump sum
Premium (annual)	$2,000	$450

Note: Both are individual policies.

Health Insurance

Peter's employer currently provides health insurance for both Peter and Patricia. The employer will continue to provide the health insurance during retirement as a benefit.

The health insurance has the following provisions:
- 80/20 coinsurance
- $2,000 family stop-loss limit
- $250 per person deductible

Disability Insurance

Neither Peter nor Patricia has disability insurance.

Homeowners Insurance

They have HO-3 policies on both the primary residence and the vacation home.

	Residence	Vacation Home
Dwelling	$600,000	$450,000
Coinsurance requirement	80%	80%
Deductible	$1,000	$500

Personal Liability Umbrella Policy

They have a $5 million personal liability umbrella policy.

Automobile Insurance

They carry the maximum liability coverage but have no comprehensive or collision coverage.

Investment Information

- They believe a $60,000 emergency fund is adequate.

- They consider themselves moderate risk takers.

- Peter's individual retirement account (IRA) investment portfolio is $600,000 of which $300,000 is invested in low-to-medium-risk equity mutual funds. Patricia is the beneficiary of the IRA and Peter's children are named as contingent beneficiaries.

- The other $300,000 of the IRA is invested in staggered maturity, short-term Treasury notes.

- Peter expects to use the income and some of the principal from the $300,000 in Treasury notes in his IRA to make up any shortfall between his retirement needs and his defined benefit plan annuity, for the period of time until Social Security benefits are received.

- Peter is currently earning an annual rate of return of 4.5% on the $300,000 invested in Treasury notes.

Income Tax Information

Peter and Patricia file a joint federal tax return but pay no state income tax. They are in the 28% marginal federal income bracket.

Retirement Information

Peter (DOB December 31, 1954)

- Has an employer-provided defined benefit plan that will pay him a joint and survivor annuity equal to 80% of a single life annuity at any retirement age of 60 or older. No reduction or increase for retirement after age 60.

- The defined benefit formula is 1.25% times the number of years of service times the final salary with no offset for Social Security. (Peter's salary for 2016 was $200,000.)

- Peter's projected Social Security benefit beginning at age 66 is $25,500 per year or approximately 75% (rounded) of that amount at age 62. Social Security benefits are expected to increase proportionally with the general inflation rate.

- Peter is expected to retire immediately, January 1, 2017. He has three options to elect regarding his defined benefit plan assets.

  — Take a lump sum distribution of $1.2 million.

  — Take a single life annuity with monthly payments taken as an annuity due beginning January 1, 2017.

  — Take a joint and survivor annuity with monthly payments taken as an annuity due beginning January 1, 2017.

Gifts, Estates, Trusts, and Will Information

Gifts

The following are all of the lifetime taxable gifts made.

1. In 1998, Peter gifted $800,000 to each of his four children. The $3,200,000 was put into an irrevocable trust. During the same year he gave $10,000 to each child (total $40,000) to use the 1998 annual exclusion. He paid gift tax of $75,000 at the time. He inherited the $3,315,000 ($3,200,000 + $40,000 + $75,000) as the primary legatee of his mother in 1998. The successor legatees were the four grandchildren (Peter's children).

2. In February 2009, Peter gave each of his four children $211,000 and paid gift tax of $59,500 at that time after application of the gift tax annual exclusion.

3. Patricia has made no taxable gifts during her lifetime.

Estates

Last illness and funeral expenses are estimated to be $5,000 and estate administration expenses are estimated to be $85,000 for each spouse.

Wills

Peter and Patricia have simple wills leaving all probate assets to one another. The debts and taxes are to be paid from the inheritance of the surviving spouse. They had the wills drafted shortly after their marriage and just prior to a vacation they took abroad. No other estate planning documents exist.

STATEMENT OF FINANCIAL POSITION
Peter and Patricia Morgan
As of January 1, 2017

Assets[1]			Liabilities and Net Worth[2]			
Cash/Cash Equivalents			**Liabilities**			
JT	Cash (money market)	$ 120,000		**Current:**		
			S1	Credit card 1	$	15,000
			S2	Credit card 2		21,000
	Total Cash/Cash Equivalents	$ 120,000	S2	Credit card 3		24,000
			S1	Auto 1 balance		30,000
			S2	Auto 2 balance		30,000
Invested Assets				Current liabilities	$	120,000
S2	Publications, Inc.	$ 900,000				
S2	Patricia's Advertising, Inc.	300,000				
S2	Patricia's investment portfolio (see detail)	270,000		**Long-term:**		
S1	Single premium deferred annuity (SPDA)	332,403		Mortgage—primary	$	450,000
S1	Peter's investment portfolio (IRA)	600,000		Mortgage—vacation		360,000
S1	Defined benefit plan (vested)	1,200,000		Long-term liabilities	$	810,000
	Total investments	$3,602,403				
Personal Use Assets				Total liabilities		930,000
JT	Primary residence[3]	900,000				
JT	Vacation home[4]	540,000				
JT	Personal property and furniture	300,000		**Net Worth**		$4,658,403
S1	Auto 1	60,000				
S2	Auto 2	66,000				
	Total Personal Use	$1,866,000				
	Total Assets	**$5,588,403**	**Total Liabilities and Net Worth**			**$5,588,403**

Notes to financial statements
[1] All assets are stated at fair market value.
[2] Liabilities are stated at principal only.
[3] Fair market value of $100,000 for the lot is included.
[4] Fair market value of $80,000 for the lot is included.

Titles and Ownership Information
S1 = Peter's separate property
S2 = Patricia's separate property
JT = Joint husband and wife (with survivorship rights)

Information Regarding Assets and Liabilities

Publications, Inc. (Patricia is the 100% shareholder of the C Corporation)

- The fair market value is $900,000.

- The original and present adjusted tax basis is $225,000 (acquired by purchase January 1, 2010).

- Patricia has agreed to sell Publications, Inc., for $900,000 on April 1, 2017. The terms are 20% down on April 1, and the balance paid in equal monthly install-ments over 10 years at 11% interest beginning on May 1, 2017.

Patricia's Advertising, Inc. (Patricia is the 100% shareholder of the C Corporation—Section 1244 stock)

- She started the business January 1, 2008, and her adjusted tax basis is $750,000.

Peter's SPDA

- The SPDA was acquired December 31, 1981, for $79,602. The current fair mar-ket value is $332,403.

- Contract had back-end surrender charges of 4.5% for the first seven years.

- Currently, the earnings rate is 6% compounded quarterly.

- The annuity start date is October 1, 2017, and will consist of quarterly annuity payments made as an annuity due over Peter's life (Peter's life expectancy is 25 years as of October 1, 2017).

- Patricia is the named beneficiary if Peter dies before the annuity start date.

Defined Benefit Plan

- The vested benefits are valued at $1.2 million.

- In the event of Peter's death before retirement benefits begin, the entire balance ($1.2 million) is paid directly to Patricia as his named beneficiary. The contin-gent beneficiaries are Peter's children.

Primary Residence

- The house was originally owned by Peter, but one-half was given to Patricia when they were married in 2011.

■ The fair market value of the residence is $900,000 (the land has a FMV of $100,000) with an adjusted tax basis of $420,000.

■ They expect to pay 6% real estate commission on any sale of the personal residence.

Vacation Home

■ The fair market value is $540,000 (the land has a FMV of $80,000).

■ The original mortgage was for 15 years at 9% with a 30% down payment.

■ The original and current payment is $4,560 per month (P & I).

■ The current mortgage balance is $360,000, with a remaining term of 120 months.

Patricia's Detailed Investment Portfolio

Description	Quantity	Fair Market Value	Beta	Years to Maturity	Annual Coupon Rate	Yearly Returns				
						16	15	14	13	12
Stock A	600	$ 18,000.00	1.15			10%	15%	12%	6%	(5%)
Stock B	1,500	$ 30,000.00	0.90			5%	6%	3%	7%	(6%)
Stock C	3,750	$ 30,000.00	0.85			5%	9%	8%	8%	(1%)
Stock D	1,200	$ 60,000.00	1.20			11%	15%	12%	10%	3%
Growth Mutual Fund	4,200	$ 63,000.00	1.15			5%	11%	14%	9%	2%
Treasury A (1 bond)	3	$ 2,788.92		2	3.75%					
Treasury B (2 bonds)	6	$ 6,151.86		3	4.25%					
Treasury C (2 bonds)	6	$ 6,816.84		5	4.5%					
Money Market		$ 53,242.38								
Total		$ 270,000.00								

Note: The correlation coefficient between Patricia's portfolio and the market is 0.9. All bonds have a par value of $1,000.

The duration of each Treasury A bond is 1.96 years; the duration of each Treasury B bond is 2.88 years; and the duration of each Treasury C bond is 4.62 years.

QUESTIONS

1. List the Morgans' financial strengths and weaknesses.

2. After reading the case, what additional information would you request from the Morgans to complete your data-gathering phase?

3. Calculate the following financial ratios for the Morgans.

$$\frac{\text{Net Worth}}{\text{Total Assets}}$$

$$\frac{\text{Total Debt}}{\text{Total Assets}}$$

4. Comment on any of the above ratios that you think are important.

5. Rounding to the nearest dollar and excluding the down payment, what is the total of the expected installment payments to be received in 2017 by Patricia from the sale of Publications, Inc.?

6. Calculate the first annuity payment from the SPDA for Peter, assuming he starts the annuity as scheduled (October 1, 2017).

7. Peter and Patricia have decided to refinance their vacation home over the remaining life of their existing current mortgage. If closing costs are paid separately, what will be the new monthly principal and interest payment?

8. Assuming Peter and Patricia sell their primary residence for the fair market value today, what are the 2017 tax consequences?

9. Peter is contemplating gifting his life insurance policy to his children, who are the current beneficiaries. What is the value of the policy for gift tax purposes?

10. In the event of a $25,000 loss due to fire on the personal residence, how much will the homeowners insurance company pay? Assume that the replacement value of the residence is $800,000.

11. You review the insurance coverage on Patricia and Peter for catastrophic coverage and estate planning. Discuss any deficiencies in their insurance coverage and estate planning.

12. What is the weighted beta of Patricia's investment portfolio based on current market values (excluding bonds and cash)?

13. With what risks should Patricia be concerned regarding her investment portfolio?

14. Patricia's current bond portfolio is not subject to which types of risk?

15. Determine which of the following bonds Patricia should purchase if she wants to increase the duration of her bond portfolio.

- Bond 1: Three-year, zero-coupon bond selling for $772.18 (Duration = 3 years)
- Bond 2: Four-year bond selling for $1,923.32 with an annual coupon payment of $375 (Duration = 2.985 years)
- Bond 3: Four-year bond selling for $983.80 with an annual coupon payment of $85 (Duration = 3.55 years)
  Note: All bonds have a par value of $1,000.

16. Is Patricia's portfolio of common stocks (including the mutual fund) subject to unsystematic risk?

17. By using the capital asset pricing model and assuming that the market yielded an annual compound rate of return of 7.4% over the past five years, has Patricia's stock portfolio, including the mutual fund, outperformed its expected return?

18. Using the Treynor ratio and the geometric mean return over the 5-year period, which of the common stocks (including the mutual fund) has the best risk-adjusted return?

19. Assuming that Patricia treats the sale of Publications, Inc., as an installment sale, what is the tax treatment for 2017 of the down payment made on April 1, 2017?

20. Rounding to the nearest dollar, calculate the amount of ordinary income and capital gain that Patricia will have in 2017 from the sale of Publications, Inc.

21. Assume that Patricia immediately sells Patricia's Advertising, Inc., for the current fair market value. What is the impact of such a transaction on the joint federal income tax return for the Morgans for 2017?

22. Assume Peter decides to withdraw $45,000 from his SPDA today, January 1, 2017. The insurance company has informed him that his quarterly annuity (ordinary) payment will be reduced to $5,735.43. What is the income tax effect of Peter's proposed withdrawal?

23. Assume that Peter begins his SPDA annuity as scheduled. What is the portion of that annuity that is includable in taxable income in 2017?

24. Calculate Peter's expected defined benefit monthly annuity payment, assuming he elects the single life annuity.

25. If Peter elects to take a lump sum distribution instead of electing an annuity, what options are available to him?

26. Calculate the annual implicit earnings rate for the single and joint life annuity payments for the defined benefit plan.

27. Peter elects to execute a trustee-to-trustee direct transfer of the lump sum benefit of his defined benefit plan into a rollover IRA. He believes he can earn 10% annually on the IRA rollover account and that inflation will equal the projected consumer price index. What single life monthly annuity in today's dollars could he create assuming the payments were made at the beginning of each month starting today? What would be the nominal payment at 10%? Should he take one of the defined benefit plan annuity payouts or the lump sum?

28. Assuming Peter decides to take Social Security retirement benefits beginning January 1, 2017, calculate his expected annual Social Security benefits for 2017.

29. If Peter died today, what would be the total of his probate estate?

30. What could Peter have done back in 1998 to avoid paying gift tax on the gifts to his four children and still have accomplished the same property transfers?

31. Are the current levels of homeowners coverage adequate on the personal residence and the vacation home? Assume the replacement values of the personal residence and vacation home are $800,000 and $460,000, respectively.

32. A person receiving Social Security benefits under full retirement age can receive income up to a maximum threshold without reducing Social Security benefits. However, there are certain types of income that do not count against the threshold. What types of income do not count against the threshold?

33. Patricia pays premiums for workers' compensation insurance for her employees at Patricia's Advertising, Inc. What are the benefits?

34. Peter and Patricia have been notified by the bank that the provisions of their loan documents require they must provide proof of physical damage coverage on their financed automobiles. Describe this coverage.

35. Peter is very fit for his age and likely to live a long time, but he has realized that Patricia is younger than his youngest child and it is unlikely much of his estate would ultimately pass to any of his children upon Patricia's death. Peter is considering an irrevocable life insurance trust (ILIT) to provide for his children. How does an ILIT work, and why is it a good choice for Peter in his estate planning?

36. What basic estate planning and will documents are missing from the Morgans' estate plan?

37. If Peter dies today, what would Patricia's options be for taking distributions from his IRA?

38. Peter and Patricia have received an unexpected offer for the vacation home of $600,000 on August 30, 2017. How much is the gain or loss on the sale of the vacation home at this price, and what are the tax implications? The house was never used as a rental by the Morgans.

39. In 1966, Robert Fortune paid $30,000 for the Fortunes' home, which included three acres of land. The home has been doubled in size over the years with $100,000 in improvements. The area has become very desirable, and the fair market value of the home was a staggering $675,000 on the date of Robert's death. Robert owned the home in his own name, and his will left his entire estate to Natalie and Patricia. Natalie and Patricia are seriously considering an offer of $750,000 for the property they received from a developer. Natalie wants to move to an assisted living complex that will offer escalated levels of care if she needs it. Several of her friends live there, and the complex provides transportation for the residents that will take Natalie wherever she wants to go. Natalie will probably need the entire proceeds of the sale to finance her move to the complex, and Patricia would like her grandmother to be able to use the entire $750,000. She has considered gifting Natalie her share of the sale proceeds ($375,000) but is concerned about the possible gift tax implications and comes to you for advice. What should you do next?

40. Assume that during a one-on-one conversation, Peter tells you he is unsure of his commitment to his marriage with Patricia. He says he is considering a divorce. He also says he hopes Patricia will waive any rights she may have in his defined benefit plan so he can take a lump-sum distribution and use it for himself post-divorce. He asks you to help convince Patricia to do so. What ethical concerns do Peter's statements present to you and how might you address them?

41. Assume that in connection with the proposed sale of Publications, Inc., Patricia is unwilling to provide you with financial information related to the company, such as tax returns, financial statements, loan agreements, and articles of incorporation. Despite your repeated requests and explanations that the information is necessary to enable you to evaluate the tax implications of the sale, she says she wants to keep this information private. What are your ethical obligations in this situation?

3

Keith and Cindy Ross

Keith and Cindy Ross have come to you, a financial planner, for help in developing a plan to accomplish their financial goals. From your initial meeting, you have gathered the following information. Assume today is January 1, 2017.

Personal Information

Keith Ross (Age 65)

Keith is in excellent health. He owns Ross Big-N-Tall, Inc., a men's store focusing on men's attire. Keith's annual salary is $250,000. Ross's employs 25 full-time and 10 part-time employees. The only debt that Keith has for the business is a $230,000 short-term loan, for which the bank required his personal guarantee.

Cindy Ross (Age 50)

Cindy is in excellent health. She is a certified public accountant and is employed by an international accounting firm, where she is currently a manager in the area of health care consulting. Her daughter from a former marriage, Beverly, is 30 years old and married with two children. Cindy's annual salary is $50,000.

The Rosses

They have been married for 25 years.

Children

Keith and Cindy have three children from their marriage.

Susie	Age 23
David	Age 21
Mary	Age 5
Beverly	Age 30 (Cindy's child from a previous marriage)

Helga Smatters

Cindy's mother, Helga, turned 71 on December 1, 2016, and is a widow with a substantial net worth. In addition to sizable holdings of real estate, stocks, and bonds, Helga has $450,000 in her individual retirement account (IRA) rollover account as of December 31, 2016 (her account grew by $25,000 during 2016). She has made no withdrawals from the IRA. Because she is in poor health, she had an attorney draft a will leaving her entire estate to Cindy. Helga would like to give to her favorite charities but has not incorporated charitable giving into her financial or estate planning. Her will provides that if Cindy should disclaim any or all of the inheritance, the disclaimed portion will be left in trust for Cindy's four children. Cindy tells you that Helga is currently the client of another financial planner, with whom she has had a planning relationship for several years.

Personal and Financial Objectives

The Rosses understand that with a large and complex estate, financial planning is an ongoing process, rather than a singular event. They would like to begin their professional relationship with you by addressing the following priorities at this time. They realize there will be additional work to address moving forward.

■ Keith wants to sell Ross Big-N-Tall and retire immediately. He believes he can sell the company within a year but is uncertain of its current value. The value shown on his Statement of Financial Position is an estimate his accountant made several years ago. He would like your opinion as to the current value of the company. The business is very stable and he wants to use last year's earnings as the basis for the valuation. As he considers purchasing a small business an aggressive investment, he wants a discount rate used in the valuation of the expected return for aggressive stocks, plus 3%.

You are one of 10 partners in a partnership that purchases small businesses it feels are undervalued and attempts to turn them around for a profit. You mention Keith's desire to sell Ross Big-N-Tall quickly to your partners, although you are sensitive to the fact that your obligation of confidentiality prevents you from disclosing any financial information about the business. Your partners tell you they believe big and tall stores have a bright future because of the national obesity epidemic and they would be interested in purchasing Keith's business if the price were right.

■ Even though the Rosses have considerable assets, they want to make a plan to secure the funding for Mary's private college education. They would like you to do an analysis to forecast costs and recommend alternatives for funding.

■ Keith and Cindy would like you to review their current estate plan and outline their greatest weaknesses. They would like to consider taking steps to improve their arrangements and welcome your input.

Economic Information

General

The Rosses expect inflation to average 3.5% annually both currently and for the long term.

U.S. Treasury Yield Curve

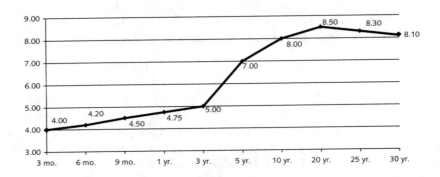

Economic Outlook—Investments

	Expected Returns	Expected Standard Deviation
Aggressive stocks	12%	15%
Growth stocks	10%	10%
S&P 500 Index	11%	8%
Corporate bonds	6%	4%
Money markets	4%	1%
90-day T-bill	4%	1%

Banking

The Rosses have favorable banking relationships and are able to borrow money for any purpose at the following rates.

Type of Loan	Rates
Installment loan—secured	7.5%
Personal signature bank loans	9.0%
Mortgage loan—30-year fixed	7.5%
Mortgage loan—15-year fixed	7.0%

Investment Information

The Rosses consider $100,000 adequate for an emergency fund. They indicate a moderate risk tolerance for investing.

Income Tax Information

The Rosses are in a marginal tax bracket of 33% for federal and 6% for state in 2016. Long-term capital gains are taxed at 15% or 20%, depending on whether any long-term capital gain realized in a given tax year raises their income above the threshold for application of the 20% rate for federal returns (no difference for state tax). Additionally, a portion of the Rosses' income may be subject to an additional 0.9% Medicare payroll tax and a 3.8% net investment income surtax on investments.

Insurance Information

Life Insurance	Policy 1	Policy 2
Insured	Keith Ross	Keith Ross
Face amount	$1,500,000	$250,000
Cash value	$175,000	$15,000
Policy type	Whole Life	Whole life
Annual premium	$12,000	$3,500
Beneficiary	Beverly, Susie, David, Mary (equally)	Cindy Ross
Contingent beneficiary	Keith's estate	Ross Children's Insurance Trust
Policyowner	Ross Children's Insurance Trust*	Cindy Ross
Interpolated terminal reserve	$175,000	$15,000
Settlement option	N/A	Single life annuity (guaranteed for 10 years)

*The original owner of Policy 1 was Keith. The policy was transferred to the trust on June 30, 2015. William Bradley, a friend of Keith's since college, is the trustee for the Ross Children's Insurance Trust. The cash value and the interpolated terminal reserve at the date of transfer was $150,000. The policy was purchased January 1, 2007.

Cindy also has group term insurance provided through her employer. She has selected $100,000 of coverage. Keith is the primary beneficiary on her group term insurance.

Health Insurance
Keith: Currently has a good health insurance plan through Ross Big-N-Tall but will not be covered once any sale of the business has been finalized. Keith's health plan has the following features.

- $1,000 individual deductible
- $2,500 family deductible
- $3,500 stop-loss limit
- 80/20 coinsurance

Cindy: Coverage is available through her employer, but she is currently covered under Keith's policy.

Disability Insurance	

Keith does not have disability insurance coverage.

Cindy has disability coverage provided through her employer: 60% gross salary, own occupation, 180-day elimination period.

Property and Liability Auto Insurance (both cars)	
Policy type	Personal auto policy
Liability (bodily injury)	$100,000/$300,000
Property damage	$50,000
Medical payments	$1,000
Physical damage, own car	Actual cash value
Uninsured motorist	$100,000/$300,000
Collision deductible	$1,000
Comprehensive deductible	$500
Annual premium (two cars)	$1,800

Homeowners Insurance	
Policy type	HO-3
Dwelling	$700,000
Other structures	$70,000
Personal property	$350,000
Personal liability	$100,000
Medical payments	$1,000
Deductible	$100
Coinsurance requirement	80%
Annual premium	$2,200

Personal Liability Umbrella Insurance

The policy has a face value of $3 million with a premium of $500 per year.

Retirement Information

Keith

- Keith has a profit-sharing plan at Ross Big-N-Tall, Inc., with a balance of $1.35 million.

- Keith also has an IRA with a balance of $30,000 (see details). The IRA was established in 1999.

■ Cindy is the beneficiary of all of Keith's retirement accounts.

■ The contingent beneficiaries on Keith's retirement accounts are Susie, David, and Mary. They are designated as equal beneficiaries.

Cindy

■ Cindy has a Section 401(k) plan in which she is able to defer up to 16% of her salary. The accounting firm matches $0.25 for each $1.00 she defers, up to 6% of her salary. The firm's total match is 1.5% of compensation. Keith is the beneficiary of all of Cindy's retirement accounts.

Keith and Cindy are retiring today. Both Keith and Cindy expect to live until age 95.

Keith and Cindy have estimated that they need $250,000 per year in today's dollars for retirement. This amount would drop by 25% if only one was alive.

Asset Allocation

The Rosses plan to create a separate portfolio to provide for their retirement income. They expect to maintain a retirement portfolio with the following asset allocation.

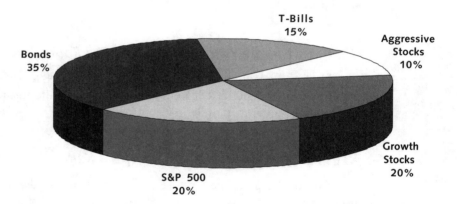

T-Bills 15%
Aggressive Stocks 10%
Bonds 35%
Growth Stocks 20%
S&P 500 20%

Education Information

Susie and David both attend Harvard. The tuition is currently $40,000 annually for each child and is expected to increase by approximately 7% per year. This cost is being funded by Keith and Cindy from current earnings and savings. They are concerned about funding Mary's education because Keith and Cindy are retiring and will not be working while Mary is in school. Mary is extremely gifted and will likely attend an Ivy League school. They expect tuition to be $40,000 annually (today's cost) and to increase by 7% each year. They expect Mary, beginning at age 18, will attend four years of undergraduate and two years of graduate school. They are inclined to begin their college savings for Mary in a bond portfolio but are open to advice on a suitable allocation for Mary's college funding needs.

Information Regarding Wills, Trusts, and Estates

Wills

Both Keith and Cindy have wills. Each of the wills provides for all of the assets to be left in a qualified terminable interest property trust with the surviving spouse as the income beneficiary and the children as the remaindermen. The Rosses believe they need to have their wills updated.

The Ross Family Irrevocable Trust

The Ross Family Irrevocable Trust was established in 2001 to reduce the Rosses' estate tax. The primary beneficiaries of the trust are the four children with the contingent beneficiary being the American Cancer Society. If a child should die, that proportional interest would pass to that child's heirs. If no heir exists, then the interest would pass equally to the remaining children of the trust. If all children should die without heirs, then the American Cancer Society would immediately receive the entire corpus of the trust. Since the trust's inception, the Rosses have made a total of $1,775,000 in taxable gifts to the trust. The gift taxes owed on the total amount was $459,000 with $148,250 allocable to gifts made in the last three years. The gift tax from last year's contribution is $90,000 and is due April 15, 2017. The trust is currently valued at $3 million.

The Ross Children's Insurance Trust (All Four Children)

This irrevocable trust was set up in early 2014 to reduce the Rosses' estate tax liability. On June 30, 2015, Keith Ross transferred life insurance Policy 1 to the trust. The trust document includes a Crummey power.

KECI Family Limited Partnership (KE = Keith; CI = Cindy; KECI = KE + CI)

One of the area's best estate planning attorneys discussed the benefits of setting up a family limited partnership with the Rosses. With his help, the Rosses established KECI Family Limited Partnership (KECI FLP) in 2013. All of the assets transferred to the FLP consisted of Keith's sole ownership property. Keith currently owns 100% of the KECI FLP but intends to begin transferring some of the ownership to his children and possibly to Cindy. The attorney has told Keith that transfers of limited partnership interests can carry a 35% overall discount for the minority interests and lack of marketability.

STATEMENT OF FINANCIAL POSITION
Keith and Cindy Ross
As of January 1, 2017

Assets[1]			Liabilities And Net Worth		
Cash/cash equivalents			**Liabilities[2]**		
S2	Cash and checking[3]	$ 20,000	S2	Credit card balances[4]	$ 15,000
S1	Cash and checking[5]	250,000	S1	Short-term loan[10]	230,000
S1	Money market fund[6]	875,000		**Total liabilities**	**$ 245,000**
	Total cash/equivalents	**$1,145,000**			
Invested assets					
S1	Profit-sharing plan—Keith	$1,350,000			
S1	IRA—Keith	30,000			
S2	Section 401(k) plan vested interest—Cindy	150,000			
S1	Growth Mutual Fund	53,100			
S1	Due from KECI	70,500			
S1	KECI Family Limited Partnership (capital)	1,193,600			
S1	Common stock portfolio[7]	100,000			
S1	Ross Big-N-Tall, Inc. Common stock[8]	2,250,000			
	Total invested assets	**$5,197,200**		**Net worth**	**$7,539,200**
Use assets					
JT	Residence[9]	$1,000,000			
JT	Personal property	400,000			
JT	Autos	42,000			
	Total use assets	**$1,442,000**			
Total assets		**$7,784,200**	**Total liabilities and net worth**		**$7,784,200**

Notes to financial statements
[1]These are presented at fair market value.
[2]All liabilities are stated at principal only. All nonidentified liabilities are jointly owned.
[3]Cindy has a POD on this account naming Keith as her beneficiary.
[4]Credit card interest rate is 18%.
[5]Cash and checking earn 1.5% annually.
[6]The money market fund earns 4% annually.
[7]Publicly traded stock.
[8]The value is an approximation of the value of the business made by Mr. Ross. The company is a C corporation with an adjusted tax basis of $25,000.
[9]Adjusted tax basis of home is $200,000 (Purchase price contributions: Keith 75% and Cindy 25%).
[10]This loan is personally guaranteed by Keith.
Title designation: S1 = Keith only; S2 = Cindy only; JT = Joint tenants with right of survivorship

STATEMENT OF CASH FLOWS
Keith and Cindy Ross
January 1, 2016 to December 31, 2016
(Expected to be similar in 2017)

INFLOWS—ANNUAL		
Keith's salary	$250,000	
Cindy's salary	50,000	
Dividend income	5,350	
Interest income	39,050	
Total inflows		$344,400
OUTFLOWS—ANNUAL		
Savings and investments	$ 56,600	$ 56,600
Fixed outflows—annual		
Property taxes	20,000	
Homeowners insurance	2,200	
Utilities	7,800	
Telephone	600	
Auto insurance	1,800	
Life insurance policies*	15,500	
Gas/oil/maintenance	1,800	
Credit card payments	8,500	
Umbrella insurance	500	$ 58,700
Variable outflows		
Taxes**	$115,114	
Food	7,800	
Medical/dental	2,000	
Clothing/personal care	6,000	
Child care	5,200	
Entertainment/vacation	10,000	
College	80,000	
Kindergarten	6,000	$232,114
Total Outflows		$347,414
Net Cash Flow (deficit)		$ ($3,014)

*Transfers to trust for life insurance Policy 1 are from net cash flow.
**Notes on taxes

FICA—Keith	$ 10,972 [($118,500 × 0.062) + ($250,000 × 0.0145)]
FICA—Cindy	3,825
Federal withholding—Keith	76,572
Federal withholding—Cindy	6,608
State—Keith	12,000
State—Cindy	3,000
.9% Additional Medicare tax—MFJ ($50,000 × .009)	450
3.8% net investment income surtax (estimated—MFJ)	$ 1,687
	$115,114

Information Regarding Assets and Liabilities

Ross Big-N-Tall, Inc.	
	Cash Flow (NOI)
Year 1	$ 400,000
Year 2	$ 420,000
Year 3	$ 435,000
Year 4 (last year)	$ 440,000
Terminal Value	$3,000,000*

*The terminal value is calculated by dividing the forecasted net operating income (NOI) for Year 5 of $450,000 by an assumed discount rate of 15%.

Detailed Investment Portfolio (These are not in the Family Limited Partnership.)

Balanced Mutual Fund				
Account Name: IRA for Keith Ross			**Account No.:** IRA4340	
Date		**Amount**	**Price/Share**	**Shares**	**Total Shares**
1/1/06	T	$16,000	$40.00	400	400
1/1/07	P	2,000	50.00	40	440
1/1/08	P	2,000	50.00	40	480
T = Transfer			P = Purchase		
Account Value as of 12/31/16				$30,000	

Note: The transfer in of $16,000 was the balance from a Section 401(k) plan with a previous employer.

Growth Mutual Fund

Fund Objective: Primarily invests in companies with market values greater than $10 billion that the fund manager believes have been undervalued by the market.

Account Name: Keith Ross   **Account No.:** SLE123456

Date	Amount	Price/Share	Shares	Total Shares
2/1/15				0
3/1/15	$7,500	$15.00	500	500
4/1/15	7,500	18.75	400	900
5/1/15	1,000	20.00	50	950
6/1/15	1,000	20.00	50	1,000
7/1/15	1,000	25.00	40	1,040
8/1/15	1,000	25.00	40	1,080
9/1/15	1,000	25.00	40	1,120
10/1/15	1,000	20.00	50	1,170
11/1/15	1,000	25.00	40	1,210
12/1/15	1,000	25.00	40	1,250
3/1/16	2,300	23.00	100	1,350
6/1/16	4,800	24.00	200	1,550
9/1/16	3,000	30.00	100	1,650
12/1/16	6,900*	27.60	250	1,900

*$2,700 was from a reinvested dividend.

Account Value as of 12/31/16: $53,100

Notes:
[1]The net asset value (NAV) of the fund on 12/31/15 was $26.00.
[2]No dividends were paid in 2015.
[3]Dividend of $1.6364 per share was paid 12/1/16.
[4]The NAV of the fund on December 31, 2016, was $27.9474.

Common Stock Portfolio

Account Name: Keith Ross

Stock	Avg./Exp. Return	Price/ Share	Total Shares	Cost Basis	Fair Market Value	Current Dividend
A	15%	$25.55	1,250.00	$ 7,500	$ 31,937.50	3%
B	13%	$37.50	850.00	$10,000	$ 31,875.00	4%
C	5%	$87.00	175.00	$18,000	$ 15,225.00	0%
D	10%	$43.00	487.50	$16,000	$ 20,962.50	2.5%
	Total			$51,500	$100,000.00	

Notes:
[1]The standard deviation of the portfolio has been 10.9% in the past and is expected to be the same in the future.
[2]The stocks purchased are as follows.

Stock A	3/5/00
Stock B	4/7/05
Stock C	6/30/15
Stock D	6/30/15

KECI Family Limited Partnership Investments

Investment	Fair Market Value	Average Expected Return	Standard Deviation	Beta
Growth and Income Mutual Fund	$ 178,000	10.0%	9%	0.92
Balanced Mutual Fund	246,500	8.5%	7%	0.72
Foreign Mutual Fund	138,500	9.7%	15%	0.30
Brokerage account A	216,000	11.2%	13%	1.22
Brokerage account B	350,000	10.4%	10%	1.12
Total investments	$1,129,000			

BALANCE SHEET
KECI Family Limited Partnership
As of January 1, 2017

ASSETS[1]

Cash/cash equivalent

Cash	$ 45,000	
Money market	55,000	
Total cash/cash equivalent		$ 100,000

Invested assets

Growth and Income Mutual Fund	$178,000	
Balanced Mutual Fund	246,500	
Foreign Mutual Fund	138,500	
Brokerage account A	216,000	
Brokerage account B	350,000	
Total invested assets		$1,129,000

Use assets[2]

Computer equipment	$ 4,000	
Luxury auto	37,500	
Depreciation[3]	(6,400)	
Total use assets		$ 35,100
Total assets		**$1,264,100**

LIABILITIES

Due to Keith Ross (on Ross Statement of Financial Position)	$ 70,500	
Total liabilities		$ 70,500
Partner's capital		$1,193,600
Total liabilities and partner's capital		$1,264,100

Notes to balance sheet
[1]All assets, other than use assets, are stated at fair market value.
[2]Use assets are listed at historical cost.
[3]Depreciation (computer = $4,000 and automobile = $2,400)

QUESTIONS

1. List the Rosses' financial strengths and weaknesses.

2. After reading the case, what additional information would you request from the Rosses to complete your data-gathering phase?

3. Ross Big-N-Tall has been profitable for the past several years. Last year net income was $440,000. If you used a discount rate of 3% above the expected return for aggressive stocks, what would be the value of the business using the capitalized earnings approach?

4. The net income in the previous year was $440,000. The income from the company can be expected to grow in the future at least at the rate of inflation. How would these additional facts affect your valuation? What model would you use to value the company?

5. Because of her financial stability and sizable net worth, Helga Smatters intends to leave the funds in her IRA untouched. When she dies, she believes that these assets will get a step-up in basis for her heirs. Comment on Helga's strategy and her beliefs and provide guidance to help her accomplish her objectives.

6. For the Growth Mutual Fund (listed on the Statement of Financial Position), what is the dollar-weighted return from March 1, 2015, to December 31, 2015?

7. Which benchmark would be the best choice to review the performance of Keith's Growth Mutual Fund?

8. What is Keith's annualized dollar-weighted return for the growth mutual fund (listed on the Statement of Financial Position) as of December 31, 2016?

9. If Keith sold the shares of the Growth Mutual Fund on January 1, 2017, what would be his after-tax annualized rate of return since he first purchased the shares?

10. If Keith needs additional cash, what would be the net proceeds from the sale of the Balanced Mutual Fund IRA (listed on his personal Statement of Financial Position), including any taxes and penalties and assuming no basis?

11. What was the gift tax valuation of the life insurance policy transferred to the Ross Children's Insurance Trust?

12. Keith's estate is the contingent beneficiary of life insurance Policy 1. What are the implications?

13. What is the implication of Keith directly paying to the insurer the future premiums for Policy 1?

14. What are the consequences if, instead of directly paying the premiums, Keith simply adds $12,000 each January 1 to the trust to pay the premiums?

15. What if Cindy assigns her coverage of the term insurance policy of $100,000 to the Ross Children's Insurance Trust?

16. How much should the Rosses set aside today for Mary's education?

17. Assuming both Keith and Cindy plan to live to age 95, how much money do the Rosses need today in their separate retirement portfolio to fund their retirement? (Assume a pretax portfolio. They will pay income taxes out of the gross retirement income.)

18. Do the Rosses have sufficient liability umbrella coverage?

19. If Keith were to die today, what assets would be included in his probate estate? Assume the Statement of Financial Position valuations.

20. If Cindy were to die today, what assets would be included in her probate estate?

21. If Keith had an objective to leave his estate to his heirs but would like to make use of the CRAT or CRUT for retirement income and the charitable tax deduction, what device could he use to replace the assets given to the CRAT or CRUT that would replace the lost assets to his heirs?

22. If Cindy attempted to disclaim her interest in Helga's estate, but for some reason the disclaimer was not effective, what would be the consequences to Cindy?

23. Assume Keith is contemplating transferring some of his wealth by making an outright gift of an interest in the KECI Family Limited Partnership as follows.

Cindy	9%
Susie	9%
David	9%
Mary	9%
Beverly	9%
	45%

Determine the amount of Keith's taxable gifts if he completes such a transaction today (2017). Assume a minority discount of 35% and that the fair market value of KECI is $1,193,600 and the annual exclusion is the same as 2016.

24. What is the weighted-average rate of return of the common stock portfolio?

25. What is the probability that Keith's common stock portfolio (listed on the Statement of Financial Position) will have a return above 0.89%?

26. Assume Keith decides to purchase a new automobile in the KECI Family Limited Partnership. The cars in KECI are used 100% for business. The car he decides to buy costs $85,000. Keith trades in his old car (listed on the KECI Statement of Financial Position) and pays cash of $55,000 from the money market account.
    a. How much gain or loss does KECI realize?
    b. How much gain is ultimately reported (recognized) on Keith's IRS Form 1040?
    c. What is the adjusted taxable basis to the partnership of the new car?

27. Cindy's mother, Helga, has gifted all four of the children with stocks and bonds over the years. Mary has $3,500 in interest income in 2016. How much of this income will be taxable to Mary after allowing for her personal exemption and standard deduction?

28. Cindy's employer paid $.25 per $1,000 each month for her group term insurance last year. The federal table rate is $.23 per $1,000 per month. Cindy contributed $6 per month toward the premium. How much of the premium the employer paid annually for her group life insurance coverage is considered W-2 income for Cindy?

29. Keith plans to sell his business and retire immediately. What effect will this have on the group health coverage he currently has for himself, Cindy, Susie, David, and Mary?

30. Helga Smatters' poor health has made the Rosses think about planning for their own care. Keith and Cindy thought Medicare would provide long-term care coverage for Helga. What coverage does Medicare provide?

31. The Rosses are reviewing their homeowners insurance coverage and have decided to have their home appraised. Their property was valued at $1.2 million of which the house was estimated to have a replacement cost of $1,050,000. Is the HO-3 coverage on the Rosses' home adequate to cover the home in case of a partial loss and, if not, what level of coverage do they need?

32. Assume that the return on Keith's common stock portfolio in 2017 is 15% and that the risk-free rate of return in 2017 is 4%. What is the Sharpe ratio for the portfolio?

33. How much must Helga withdraw from her IRA for the year 2016 to avoid a tax penalty? Use the appropriate divisor from the following table to calculate your answer.

Age	Applicable Divisor
70	27.4
71	26.5
72	25.6

34. Describe any possible weaknesses you see in the coverage of the Rosses' personal property under their homeowners policy. What solutions are available that might address these weaknesses?

35. If Helga dies in 2017 and Cindy is the designated beneficiary of her IRA, what options are available to Cindy for taking distributions from the IRA?

36. What is the beta of Keith's common stock portfolio? Assume that the standard deviation of the market is 8% and the correlation coefficient between the portfolio and the market is 0.75.

37. What ethical concerns, if any, are raised by your involvement in the partnership that purchases small businesses, and what must you do to address them?

38. Assume that during your planning engagement with the Rosses, Helga Smatters calls you and asks you several questions about the Rosses' financial plans. You reply that the Rosses' plans are not yet finalized but that generally their plans are to sell Keith's business and retire. You promise to call her back when their plans are further along. You also tell Helga that Cindy has mentioned some of her estate planning goals to you and you have recommendations that might help her achieve them. You say that you recently completed some training on new estate planning techniques and that your knowledge is more advanced that most other planners in the area. You suggest that if Helga made an appointment with you, you would be able to begin working on a plan together. What ethical concerns are raised by your conversation with Helga?

39. Keith and Cindy have come to you to discuss assisting with college education funding for Beverly's two children, Cindy's grandchildren. The children are close in age to their daughter, Mary, and the Rosses believe now is the time to start college savings. What should you do next?

4

Karl and June Monroe

Karl and June Monroe have come to you, a financial planner, for help in developing a plan to accomplish their financial goals. From your initial meeting, you have gathered the following information. Assume today is January 1, 2017.

Personal Background and Information

Karl Monroe (Age 37)

Karl is the owner and manager of a bar named Marlo's. Marlo's is a small, neighborhood bar that is open only at nights and has five part-time employees (less than 1,000 hours each). Karl inherited the bar four years ago from his Uncle Marlo. Karl attended Arizona State University and received an MBA in management. After graduation, he became employed by Texas Energy Resources, Inc., an oil and gas exploration company based in Austin, Texas, where he served as their human resources manager. The company paid for Karl to attend graduate school at the University of Texas-Austin. He attended classes part-time at night and earned his MBA. He was earning $78,500 when he inherited the bar. Because of the volatility in the oil and gas industry, Karl felt that Marlo's afforded him a more stable working environment and a chance for self-employment. He decided to leave Texas Energy Resources, Inc., and dedicate all his efforts to Marlo's.

June Monroe (Age 37)

June is a loan officer at Wood National Bank. She has been employed by Wood for eight years. She attended Texas Christian University and received her BA in finance. She also attended the University of Texas-Austin and earned her MBA. June and Karl resided in an apartment in Austin when Karl was transferred to San Antonio by Texas Energy Resources, Inc. June transferred to San Antonio and maintained her position at the Wood National Bank in San Antonio.

The Monroes

Karl and June have been married for 11 years. They both plan to retire in 25 years. They own a three-bedroom house with a pool, two cars, and a bar (Marlo's) in San Antonio, Texas. They have three children and do not plan on having any more children.

The Children

Sebastian, age 10, attends Davy Crockett Grammar School (the local public school) and is in the fourth grade.

Sandy, age 5, also attends Davy Crockett Grammar School and is in kindergarten. Sandy spends the afternoon at Alamo Day Care Center.

April, age 2, attends Alamo Day Care Center for nine hours a day, Monday through Friday.

The Grandparents

Karl's mother, Gerdi, age 62, was widowed four years ago when her husband died at age 60. Her only income is $600 a month from Social Security and $500 a month from Karl and June. She does not spend the $600 from Social Security; she deposits it in her money market account. She lives about 100 miles from Karl and June.

June's mother, Maria, age 70, is a lifelong resident and citizen of Colombia and is fully supported by Karl and June. Karl and June contribute $300 each month to support Maria.

Personal and Financial Objectives

The Monroes have the following financial objectives in order of priority.

1. They want to provide a standard of living after retirement of 80% of their preretirement earnings. The Monroes stated they are comfortable assuming an 11% investment annual rate of return in retirement needs analysis calculations.

2. They want to accumulate sufficient assets to send the children to a state university away from home, yet in the state of Texas.

3. They want to minimize their current income tax liability.

4. They want to expand Marlo's to include a daytime grill within the next five years.

5. They want to be mortgage free at retirement.

6. They want to develop an estate plan to minimize estate tax liabilities.

Economic Information

- The Monroes expect inflation to average 3% annually, both currently and for the long term. They also expect June's salary to increase 5% annually, both currently and long term.

- Current mortgage rates are 7.5% for 15 years and 8.0% for 30 years. Closing costs would be 3% of the amount financed and would be paid at closing.

Insurance Information

Life Insurance

	Policy 1	Policy 2
Insured	June	Karl
Policy through	Employer	State Lake
Face amount	$50,000	$150,000
Policy type	Term (group)	Whole
Cash value	$0	$21,250*
Annual premium	$102 (employer paid)	$2,361
Beneficiary	Karl	June
Contingent beneficiary	Three children (equally)	None
Policyowner	June	Karl**
Settlement option	None	Life Annuity

*Karl's after-tax earnings rate is 6%. Cash value at January 1 last year was $20,900, and last year's dividend was $100.
**Community property

June also has an accidental death and dismemberment policy through her employer. She is covered for $100,000 under this policy. She pays a premium of $68 per year for this coverage.

Health Insurance

All family members are covered by June's employer under a group health plan with an annual family deductible of $400. After the deductible is met, the plan pays 100% of the first $2,000 of covered hospital charges for each hospital stay and 80% thereafter. The policy features a $2,000 maximum out-of-pocket limit. The plan will then pay 100% of any other covered expenses.

Dental Insurance

The Monroes have dental insurance. The premium is $216 annually.

Disability Insurance

Karl has a personal disability policy with an own-occupation definition that provides a benefit of $2,000 per month after a 30-day elimination period. The policy was purchased from a local insurance company. This policy covers both accidents and sickness and has a benefit period of five years. His annual premium is $608.

June has an own-occupation definition policy that provides a benefit of 65% of gross pay after a 90-day elimination period. The policy is provided through her employer. The policy covers both accidents and sickness until age 65. The annual premium is $460, and the employer and June each pay half.

Homeowners Insurance

The Monroes have a HO-3 policy (replacement value) with a $250 deductible, a dwelling value of $97,000, an 80% coinsurance requirement, and a current yearly premium of $739. There is a $100,000 liability coverage per occurrence.

Automobile Insurance

The Monroes own one vehicle and lease the other. They carry the same automobile coverage on both vehicles.

Both Cars	
Policy type	Personal Auto Policy
Liability	$100,000/$300,000
Medical payments	$5,000 per person
Physical damage, own car	Actual cash value
Uninsured motorist	$50,000/accident
Collision deductible	$100
Comprehensive deductible	$250
Premium (per year)	$1,080

The Honda was leased (two-year lease beginning January 1, 2015, and expiring December 31, 2016) with no purchase option. June has no plans to renew the lease because she prefers to drive a newer car as she believes they are more reliable. She will lease a 2017 model Honda in January 2017.

Investment Data

The Monroes' tolerance for investment risk on a scale of 1 to 10 (1 being the most risk averse) is a 7. They expect to be more conservative as they get closer to retirement.

Income Tax Information

Their marginal income tax rate is currently 25% for federal income taxes, and there are no state income taxes in Texas.

Retirement Information

The Monroes plan to retire in 25 years when they are 62 years old. They would like to have a standard of living equal to 80% of their preretirement income. At or before retirement, the Monroes plan to sell the bar and put the proceeds toward retirement. They expect to be in retirement for 28 years.

June has a Section 401(k) plan through Wood National Bank. Wood matches $1 for every $4 contributed up to an employer maximum contribution of 2% of salary. The maximum employee contribution without regard to the match is 10% of salary. She has been contributing 5% of her salary since she began working there in 2004. Her account has averaged an annual rate of return of 7% over the past eight years. Her estate is currently designated as the beneficiary.

Karl has an individual retirement account (IRA) through his banker. He opened the account 10 years ago and has been contributing $3,000 each year since 2011. Before 2011, he contributed $2,000 annually. He has averaged a 6% annual rate of return over the past 10 years. He always contributes on January 1 of the year in question. His estate is the beneficiary of the IRA.

Karl expects to collect $23,856 in Social Security benefits at age 67 or 70% of full retirement benefits at age 62 (in today's dollars). June expects to collect $22,840 in Social Security benefits at age 67 and 70% at age 62 (in today's dollars). They expect to begin receiving Social Security benefits as soon as they retire.

Gifts, Estates, Trusts, and Will Information

The Monroes have simple wills leaving all probate assets to one another.

STATEMENT OF CASH FLOWS
Karl and June Monroe
For the Year Ended December 31, 2016 (and projected for 2017)

INFLOWS

Karl's net income from the bar (Schedule C)	$64,000	
June's salary	57,200	
Dividend income	777	
Checking interest income	130	
Savings interest income	400	
Certificate of deposit	275	
Total inflows		**$122,782**

OUTFLOWS
Planned savings

Section 401(k) plan 5% deferral for June	$ 2,860	
IRA	3,000	
Total planned savings		**$ 5,860**

Ordinary living expenses

Mortgage (principal and interest)	$10,267	
Homeowners insurance premium	739	
Church donations—cash	5,200	
Lease on Honda	3,588	
Principal and interest on Cherokee	7,800	
Gas/oil/maintenance	2,000	
Auto insurance payments (both cars)	1,080	
Credit card payments	6,200	
Taxes on income	41,018	
Property taxes on residence	2,657	
Utilities	1,200	
Telephone	600	
Life insurance premiums (Karl)	2,361	
Accidental death and dismemberment	68	
Support for Gerdi and Maria	9,600	
Health	2,592	
Dental insurance	216	
Child care (paid to Alamo)	4,500	
Disability income insurance premiums (both)	838	
Vacation expense	4,000	
Entertainment expense	3,250	
Food	3,250	
Clothing	3,000	
Total ordinary living expenses		**$116,024**
Total outflows		**$121,884**
Net cash flow (Surplus)		**$ 898**

NOTES REGARDING TAXES

FICA—Karl ($64,000 × .9235 x .153)	$9,043
FICA—June (7.65% × $57,200)	4,375
Estimated payments (Karl)	12,600
Federal withholding (June)	15,000
Total taxes	$41,018

STATEMENT OF FINANCIAL POSITION
Karl and June Monroe
January 1, 2017

Assets[1]			Liabilities and Net Worth[2]	
Cash/cash equivalents			**Current Liabilities**	
Checking account (2.5%)	CP	$ 5,200	Credit card balances (14.7%)	$ 8,200
Savings account (3.25%)[3]	CP	12,300	Car loan (Jeep Grand Cherokee)	11,000
Total cash/cash equivalents		$ 17,500	Total current liabilities	19,200
Invested assets			**Long-term liabilities**	
Certificate of deposit	CP	$ 5,000	Home mortgage	$ 98,836
(5.5%, 2 year, matures 12/31/17)			(9.25% for 30 years)	
Saving bonds	CP	4,000	Total long-term liabilities	$ 98,836
(Zero-coupon EE bonds)	CP			
Mutual funds	CP	18,800		
Stocks	CP	13,600		
Section 401(k) plan vested balance (June)	CP	31,331	**TOTAL LIABILITIES**	$118,036
IRA (Karl)	CP	27,942		
Proprietorship in bar	CP	138,000		
Rental property	S2	84,000		
Cash value life insurance	CP	21,250		
Total investments		$343,923		
			NET WORTH	$402,787
Personal use assets				
House[4] (land has a FMV of $20,000)	CP	$125,000		
Jewelry (one diamond)	CP	8,000		
Jeep Grand Cherokee	CP	24,000		
Baseball card collection	S1	2,400		
Total personal use		$159,400		
TOTAL ASSETS		**$520,823**	**TOTAL LIABILITIES AND NET WORTH**	**$520,823**

Notes to financial statements

[1]Assets are stated at fair market value.
[2]Liabilities are stated at principal only and are all community obligations.
[3]The savings account is currently serving as their emergency fund.
[4]Replacement value is $105,000.

General note: The numbers in parentheses reflect the interest that is being assessed.

Title designations

CP = Community property
S1 = Karl's separate property
S2 = June's separate property

Information Regarding Assets and Liabilities

Marlo's

Marlo's is located one block off the local college campus and has been in business for 32 years. Marlo had a taxable basis in the bar of $10,000 at his death. The fair market value at the time of Marlo's death was $40,000. Two years ago, Karl executed a legal document making Marlo's community property with June.

Karl completely refurbished the bar at a cost of $30,000. The building and property are currently valued at $78,000. Property taxes are high in this district; they are currently $2,278 (2.92 per hundred). The bar could be sold at a fair market value of $138,000 and is increasing at 3.5% per year. The bar's net income for the last three years was $64,000, $59,600, and $57,500.

They also expect Karl's net income from Marlo's to increase at 3.5% annually, both currently and over the long term.

Personal Residence

The Monroes purchased their home and financed the mortgage over 30 years at 9.25%. The house is a two-story, three-bedroom, brick house with a pool and a monitored burglar alarm.

Rental Property

The rental property, which is valued at $84,000, is located in Austin, Texas, and consists of a small strip shopping center. The center is in a poor location and is currently a break-even proposition as income equals expenses. The property was acquired from June's Aunt Grace three years ago as a gift. Grace's basis in the property was $20,000 ($5,000 for the land and $15,000 for the building) and she paid gift tax of $24,000 on the transfer. At the time of the gift, the property had a fair market value of $60,000. Grace died recently, and at the time of her death the property was valued at $84,000.

Prior to Grace's death, June and Karl would never dispose of the rental property for fear of offending Grace; however, they now want to buy a strip shopping center in San Antonio at a cost of $100,000 by using a small mortgage of $16,000. A tenant in the Austin property would consider buying the rental property for the fair market value of $84,000.

An old friend of yours is a real estate investor in Austin. You mention the Monroes' strip mall to him and ask him whether he knows what the property might be worth. He says one of his friends in state government has told him that the highway commission plans to purchase the property for $125,000 within the next couple of years as part of a new highway project going through the neighborhood. He tells you he is willing to pay the Monroes $90,000 for the property if you will connect him with them and, if the state does buy the property, he will give you one-third of his profits.

Mutual Funds

	Fair Market Value	Beta	Expected Return
Balanced Fund	$ 5,600	0.65	8.5%
Growth Fund	2,400	1.24	12.4%
Corporate Bond Fund	10,800	0.55	6.5%
Total	**$18,800**		

QUESTIONS

1. List the Monroes' financial strengths and weaknesses.

2. After reading the case, what additional information would you request from the Monroes, and what actions would you take to complete your data-gathering phase?

3. Calculate the following financial ratios for the Monroes.

$$\frac{\text{Liquid Assets}}{\text{Monthly Expenses}}$$

$$\frac{\text{Liquid Assets}}{\text{Current Debt Payments}}$$

$$\frac{\text{Net Worth}}{\text{Total Assets}}$$

$$\frac{\text{Total Debt}}{\text{Total Assets}}$$

$$\frac{\text{Total Debt}}{\text{Annual Total Income*}}$$

$$\frac{\text{Housing and Monthly Debt Payments}}{\text{Monthly Gross Income}}$$

$$\frac{\text{Housing Costs}}{\text{Monthly Gross Income}}$$

$$\frac{\text{Investment Assets}}{\text{Annual Gross Income}}$$

$$\frac{\text{Monthly Savings}}{\text{Monthly Gross Income}}$$

*Annual Total Income is the same as Annual Gross Income.

4. Comment on any of the above ratios that you think are important.

5. Assuming the Monroes have always made their mortgage payments exactly as agreed, how much was their original mortgage?

6. Assuming the Monroes have always made their mortgage payments exactly as agreed, how many payments have the Monroes made on the mortgage?

7. Do the Monroes qualify to refinance their mortgage?

8. If they refinance, how much will they save over the life of the mortgage for a 15-year or 30-year mortgage? Which mortgage should they select?

9. What other method might they consider to save on the repayment of the mortgage?

10. Is their health care insurance coverage adequate?

11. How much qualified residence interest can they deduct on their income tax return for last year?

12. Was Gerdi a dependent of the Monroes for income tax purposes last year? Explain why or why not.

13. Was Maria a dependent of the Monroes for income tax purposes last year? Explain why or why not.

14. How much of a dependent care credit, if any, can the Monroes take for 2016?

15. For 2016, can Karl make a deductible contribution to an individual retirement account (IRA) as an alternative to or as an addition to any qualified plan he may implement?

16. Estimate the Monroes' federal adjusted gross income for last year.

17. Because Marlo's is a sole proprietorship, which types of retirement plans can Karl establish?

18. What type of retirement plan should Karl adopt if he wishes to maximize contributions and minimize his cash commitment?

19. What is the maximum contribution Karl can make to a qualified defined contribution plan in the current year?

20. What would be the impact on the Monroes' federal income tax liability for this year if Karl were to establish a Keogh and maximize his contributions? (Assume his Schedule C income is the same as last year.)

21. Discuss Karl's ability to have a loan provision if he establishes a Keogh plan.

22. What is the projected value of Marlo's at Karl's expected retirement date? (Use the current Statement of Financial Position valuation.)

23. Calculate the Monroes' capital needed at retirement. Assume an earnings rate of 11%.

24. Calculate the capital needed at retirement for the Monroes by using the annuity approach.

25. Calculate the capital needed at retirement for the Monroes by using the capital preservation approach. Assume an earnings rate of 11%.

26. Calculate the capital needed at retirement for the Monroes by using the purchasing power preservation approach.

27. Explain the differences between the capital preservation model and the purchasing power preservation model.

28. Can June make an in-service withdrawal from her Section 401(k) plan if Marlo's needs cash flow?

29. Can June's Section 401(k) plan have a loan provision?

30. Gerdi is considering going back to work and wants to know how much she can earn before she will lose any Social Security benefits. How much will she have to make to lose all benefits?

31. What are the income tax consequences of any disability benefits received by Karl and June?

32. Discuss the strengths and weaknesses of disability benefits for Karl and June.

33. Is the life insurance amount adequate for Karl and June?

34. Is the homeowners insurance coverage appropriate?

35. Analyze the Monroes' liability insurance coverage.

36. What are the federal income tax consequences of a sale of the Austin rental property if the Monroes had taken $4,308 as a depreciation deduction for the property?

37. If, instead of a sale of the Austin property, June uses a tax-free exchange to acquire the San Antonio shopping center, what is her recognized gain or loss from the Austin property and her basis in the new property?

38. What is Karl and June's adjusted tax basis in Marlo's?

39. If Karl were to die today and June inherited and sold Marlo's for the current Statement of Financial Position value, what would be her income-adjusted basis at the time of the sale?

40. What is the expected return for the Monroes' mutual fund portfolio?

41. What is the weighted beta for the Monroes' mutual fund portfolio?

42. Consider the following modern portfolio theory statistics for the growth fund.

	1st Index	2nd Index	3rd Index
R^2	0.67	0.56	0.98
Beta	0.95	1.0	1.3
Alpha	1.2	3.25	0.05

Which of the indexes is the appropriate benchmark for the growth fund?

43. Assume that the Monroes want to invest $10,000. They decide to invest $7,000 in Portfolio A with the remainder in the S&P 500. Changes in the S&P 500 account for 25% of the returns for Portfolio A. If Portfolio A has a standard deviation of 20% and the S&P 500 has a standard deviation of 11.5%, what is the standard deviation of the combined $10,000 portfolio?

44. Because they have little cash flow available to save for the children's college educations, the Monroes have asked you to determine if the projected net income on the San Antonio strip mall purchase should be invested for college funding. What do you do next?

45. What estate planning deficiencies do the Monroes have?

46. What is the total of all the assets that will be included in Karl's probate estate if he were to die today?

47. What could be done to reduce Karl's probate estate?

48. What ethical concerns, if any, are raised by your conversation with your old friend, the real estate investor in Austin, about the Monroes' rental property and what must you do to address them?

49. Assume that as part of your planning recommendations to the Monroes, you recommend that they implement an estate planning devoted to the avoidance of federal estate tax. Your recommendations include the execution of complex wills incorporating bypass planning and QTIP trusts. The Monroes accept your recommendations and an attorney employed by your firm drafts the necessary documents for the Monroes at a total cost of $4,000. What ethical concerns are raised by this scenario?

5

Benjamin and Sarah Redding

Benjamin and Sarah Redding have great aspirations for their future. They have only recently realized that they are not as financially secure as they had originally thought. They have come to you for advice on how to solve their current cash flow issues and to help them make plans to achieve their goals. Today is January 1, 2017.

Personal Background and Information

Benjamin Redding (Age 30)

Benjamin Redding graduated from a state university seven years ago with a bachelor of science degree in accounting. He has been employed for almost seven years at Moore & Moore, a small accounting firm (50 employees).

Benjamin has been married to Sarah Steiner Redding for six years.

Sarah Steiner Redding (Age 29)

Sarah Steiner Redding grew up in a wealthy family. She graduated from a private university with a bachelor of science degree in elementary education. She is employed as a fourth grade teacher at a private school, Woodridge Preparatory School, and has been for the past five years. To further enrich her students (and for additional income), Sarah tutors three students each week. She incurs no expenses when providing this tutoring.

Children

Benjamin and Sarah have three children: Scott, age 4, and twin girls, Janice and Carly, age 1.

Delores Vidalia

The Reddings employ a young student, Delores Vidalia, to care for their children. Delores, age 21, is a part-time night student at a local community college. She cares for the children and cleans the Reddings' house in exchange for room, board, and a $100 stipend per week. The Reddings pay Delores in cash. Neither the Reddings nor Dolores report these transactions to the IRS. Delores works 48 weeks per year.

Benjamin's Family

George Redding married Julie Redding in 1985. They had two children, George Jr., and Benjamin. George Jr., died at age six months of sudden infant death syndrome.

Benjamin's father, George Sr., died of a heart attack six years ago at age 50. He had ample insurance to cover all medical and funeral expenses.

His mother, Julie, a chain-smoker for 37 years, is 53 years old. She was diagnosed with lung cancer three years ago. Because of her rapidly deteriorating health, her doctor has predicted that she probably will not live beyond five to seven years. She is receiving monthly chemotherapy treatments at a medical center ($200 out-of-pocket cost per visit).

Her doctor has recommended that she be placed in a home with 24-hour care as soon as possible. The cost of this care, including room and board, is about $175 per day, or approximately $5,323 per month. Because of her increased medical expenses and need for constant care, Julie has decided to sell her home. She has contacted Jane Smith, a real estate agent, who has listed her home for $140,000. Julie is adamant that she will accept no less than $135,000.

Benjamin and Sarah have been giving Julie $200 per month to help ease her financial burden. They will be forced to incur most of her future expenses. They realize that the sale of the home will provide some assistance; however, the real estate market is soft, and they have had no offers on the house. Julie owns a paid-up whole life insurance policy on her own life with a face amount of $500,000 and a cash surrender value (CSV) of $75,000. The policy is not a modified endowment contract (MEC).

Benjamin's Great Aunt Mabel plans to give Benjamin and Sarah $10,000 each at the beginning of 2017. Benjamin has always looked out for Mabel, and she wants to show him her gratitude through this gift.

Sarah's Family

Harry Steiner III married Alice Steiner in 1972. Sarah is an only child and the Steiners' pride and joy.

Harry Steiner is a highly respected State Supreme Court justice. He has worked in the city for more than 30 years and is considered an extremely influential figure in the community. Harry and Alice's adjusted gross income (AGI) exceeds $275,000.

Alice Steiner was born into a wealthy family. Before they were married, she and Harry decided that she would not work. She is, however, very active in the community through her volunteer work four days a week.

The Steiners were happy to welcome Benjamin into their family. In fact, Harry was so excited that he presented Benjamin with a speedboat in hopes that he would get to spend time on the boat getting to know his future son-in-law. As a wedding gift, the Steiners gave Sarah and Benjamin $20,000 toward the purchase of a new home.

In addition, the Steiners set up a $100,000 trust fund to assist their grandchildren with college education expenses. Sarah, the beneficiary of the trust fund, receives the monthly interest from the principal until the trust is dissolved, with first Benjamin and then Children's Hospital as successor beneficiaries in the event of Sarah's death. Upon Scott's enrollment in college, he will be given his third of the trust fund, $33,333. Sarah will continue to receive the interest on the remaining $66,666 until Janice and Carly begin college. If a child should die or decide not to go to college by age 22, that child's share would be donated to Children's Hospital.

Benjamin was previously married to Carol, an attorney, and together they had one child, Stephen. Benjamin pays Carol $500 each month for child support. Carol's parents have agreed to pay 100% of Stephen's college tuition and expenses.

Personal and Financial Objectives

The Reddings listed the following financial objectives in direct order of importance to their family.

1. Provide private education for all three children at Woodridge Preparatory School for grades K–12.

2. Provide each child with up to $15,000 per year for college education for up to four years in addition to the trust fund.

3. Assist Julie with living and medical expenses until her death.

4. Purchase a home for $300,000 in eight years with a 20% down payment. (By that time, Benjamin should be a partner of the firm.) Housing costs are expected to increase with inflation. They intend to keep their current home as a rental property.

5. Be free of mortgage indebtedness by the time Benjamin is 55 years old.

6. Prepare a proper retirement plan allowing them a debt-free retirement. They feel that income of $75,000 in today's dollars per year will allow them to maintain their standard of living.

7. Rebuild their savings account/emergency fund to a minimum of $25,000.

8. Save for the twins' future weddings (estimated costs $15,000 each).

Economic Information

- They expect inflation to average 4% annually.

- They expect Sarah's salary to increase each year by 5%.

- They expect Benjamin's salary to increase each year by 5%.

- Mortgage rates are 5.5% for a 15-year fixed and 6.0% for a 30-year fixed. Any refinancing will incur 3% of the mortgage amount as a closing cost.

Insurance Information

Health Insurance

An HMO health insurance plan is provided for the entire family by Moore & Moore. Doctor visits are $10 per visit, while prescriptions are $5 for generic brands and $10 for other brands. There is no co-payment for hospitalization in semiprivate accommodations. Private rooms are provided when medically necessary. For emergency treatment, a $50 co-payment is required.

Life Insurance

Benjamin has a $110,000 group term life insurance policy through Moore & Moore. Highly compensated employees of Moore & Moore receive group term coverage in the amount of five times their salaries. Sarah has a $27,000 group term life insurance policy through Woodridge Preparatory School. The owners of the policies are Benjamin and Sarah, respectively, with each other as the beneficiary.

Disability Insurance

Benjamin has disability insurance through Moore & Moore. Short-term disability benefits begin for any absence due to sickness and accident more than six days and will continue for up to six months at 80% of his salary. Long-term disability benefits are available if disability continues more than six months. If Benjamin is unable to perform the major and substantial duties of his current occupation, the coverage provides him with 60% of his salary while disabled until recovery, death, retirement, or age 65 (whichever occurs first). All disability insurance premiums are fully paid by Moore & Moore.

Sarah has no disability insurance.

Professional Liability Insurance

Moore & Moore has professional liability insurance covering all employees.

Homeowners Insurance

The Reddings have an HO-3 policy with a $140,000 dwelling coverage limit and liability coverage of $100,000 endorsed to provide loss settlement on a replacement cost basis for personal property. Dwelling coverage is provided on an open peril basis and personal property coverage is provided on a named peril basis. The deductible is $500 with an annual premium of $750.

Automobile Insurance

Benjamin and Sarah have the following coverage on both cars:

- $100,000 bodily injury per person;
- $300,000 bodily injury aggregate;
- $50,000 property damage;
- $100,000 uninsured motorist per person; and
- $300,000 uninsured motorist aggregate.

Deductibles are:

- $500 comprehensive (no deductible for glass); and
- $1,000 collision.

This insurance includes medical payments, car rentals, and towing. The cost of the auto insurance is $3,260.50 per year because of two at-fault accidents Sarah has caused in the past three years.

Investment Information (Prospective)

	Expected Return	Beta
Aggressive stocks	13%	1.6
Growth stocks	10%	1.1
S&P 500 Index	9%	1.0
Corporate bonds	7%	0.5
Money market (bank)	2%	0.3

The Reddings consider themselves to be moderate risk investors.

Income Tax Information

The Reddings are in the 15% marginal income tax bracket. Their combined marginal income tax bracket (federal and state) is 18%.

Retirement Information

Benjamin and Sarah would both like to retire when they are 65 and 64 years old, respectively, and they expect to be in retirement for 30 years. They would hope to have $75,000 per year of pretax income in today's dollars during retirement. They do not want to rely on Social Security benefits for their retirement planning. Any money received from Social Security will be considered extra income.

Benjamin does not participate in the Section 401(k) plan available through Moore & Moore. In the plan, the firm matches $.50 for every dollar contributed, up to 6% of his contribution (if he contributes 6% of his salary, the company contributes 3%). Benjamin may defer a maximum of 16% of his salary.

Sarah is enrolled in a defined contribution plan in which the school contributes 7% of her salary and she contributes 3%. The plan provides several investment options: bond funds, stock funds, and money market accounts. She has chosen to invest this contribution in fixed instruments (bond funds). The plan has a 2- to 6-year graduated vesting schedule, and she has been a participant for four years. The total balance of her account is $16,500. Although she has not participated, she also has available a Section 403(b) supplemental retirement plan to which she may contribute up to 13% of her salary.

Gifts, Estates, Trusts, and Will Information

Presently, neither Benjamin nor Sarah have wills; however, both realize the importance of having them. They would like to create wills leaving everything to one another and the children, while minimizing the impact of both estate and gift taxes.

STATEMENT OF CASH FLOWS
Benjamin and Sarah Redding
2016
(Expected to be the same for 2017)

CASH INFLOWS

Salary—Benjamin	$55,000.00	
Salary—Sarah	27,000.00	
Tutoring—Sarah[1]	3,600.00	
Interest—trust	3,000.00	
Savings account withdrawal[2]	5,569.80	
Total inflows		$94,169.80

CASH OUTFLOWS

Defined contribution plan—Sarah	$ 810.00	
Mortgage payment (principal and interest)	12,798.24	
Property taxes (residence)	1,250.00	
FICA	6,273.00	
Federal withholding	11,078.20	
State withholding	903.95	
Utilities	5,400.00	
Homeowners insurance	750.00	
Auto note	6,374.16	
Auto expense/maintenance	3,490.00	
Auto insurance	3,260.50	
Child care/House care[3]	4,800.00	
Education loans[4]	2,892.60	
Credit card payments[5]	2,170.08	
Bank loans[6]	7,251.25	
Dry cleaning	900.00	
New clothing	3,550.00	
Food	6,000.00	
Dining out/entertainment	3,600.00	
Miscellaneous	3,600.00	
Child support payment to Carol	6,000.00	
Total Outflows		$93,151.98
Net Cash Flow (Surplus)		$ 1,017.82

Notes to Financial Statements
[1]Sarah does not report this money to the IRS.
[2]$366 is earned interest.
[3]The Reddings pay the maid in cash and do not report it to the IRS.
[4]$1,643 is interest, the balance is principal.
[5]The Reddings pay the minimum monthly payment on credit cards.
[6]$4,350 is interest, the balance is principal.

STATEMENT OF FINANCIAL POSITION
Benjamin and Sarah Redding
January 1, 2017

ASSETS[1]

Checking account	$ 10,000	
Savings account	13,500	
Trust fund[2]	100,000	
Automobile—Sarah (2007 BMW 328i)	12,575	
Automobile—Benjamin (2015 Nissan Maxima)	16,375	
Boat	12,000	
Home (appraised 7/1/16)	149,000	
Pension—Sarah	16,500	
Total assets		$329,950

LIABILITIES[3,4]

Credit card—Benjamin (18%)	$ 4,750	
Credit card—Sarah (23%)	4,920	
Credit card—joint (16%)	1,200	
Car loan—Benjamin (10%)	18,383	
Student loans (6%)	17,919	
Bank loans (12%)	9,909	
Home mortgage balance (7.5%)	148,944	
Total liabilities		$206,025
Net worth		$123,925
Total liabilities and net worth		$329,950

Notes to Financial Statements
[1]All assets are stated at fair market value.
[2]The trust fund is for the children's education; however, Sarah receives the interest on the balance of the trust fund until all children reach age of majority. The trust assets are invested in a CD yielding 3% per year.
[3]Liabilities are stated at principal only.
[4]Percentages shown (%) are current interest rates on respective indebtedness.

Information Regarding Assets and Liabilities

Employment

Benjamin is currently employed as a senior accountant at Moore & Moore, earning an annual salary of $55,000. He expects to be promoted to manager within two years. Benjamin hopes to be a partner in eight years.

Sarah earns $27,000 annually teaching at Woodridge Preparatory School. Annual salary increases range from 3–5%. She also earns approximately $3,600 each year tutoring. This money is received in cash. Although they should, she and Benjamin do not report her tutoring earnings on their tax returns. In addition, Sarah receives $3,000 a year, before taxes, on the interest earned from the children's trust fund.

Benjamin and Sarah earn approximately 2% interest on their savings account. This is automatically credited on a quarterly basis to the account; however, they do not consider this small amount of interest to be income. This savings account/emergency fund began with an account balance of $25,000 when they were first married. In 2016, they withdrew $366 in interest income and $5,203.80 from the savings account to pay bills.

Home

Benjamin and Sarah purchased a four-bedroom house for $170,000 in a nice family neighborhood. They were among the first families to purchase a home in this new subdivision. The money received from Sarah's parents as a wedding gift was used for the down payment. The mortgage payment is $1,066.52 per month. The interest rate is 7.5%. The original mortgage was $152,531.47, and they have made 29 payments. Utilities range from $400–500 per month.

Although the original value of the house was $170,000, a recent appraisal valued the house at $149,000. The decrease in value did not leave enough equity for the Reddings to be approved for a home equity loan. If the Reddings wanted to refinance (80% of the fair market value of the home), the 3% closing costs would have to be paid at closing and not financed.

Automobiles

In 2015, Benjamin purchased a new Nissan Maxima for $25,000. The current value of the car is $16,375, but the loan balance is $18,383.47. The term of the loan is 60 months at 10% interest. Benjamin has made 19 monthly payments of $531.18.

Sarah won a new 2007 BMW 328i in a contest. The car has a current value of $12,575.

Boat

The current value of Benjamin's 18-foot boat with a 150 HP Mercury is $12,000. Though Benjamin and Sarah consider this a luxury item, they know that the sale of the boat may harm their relationship with Sarah's parents.

Student Loans

Benjamin put himself through school with part-time jobs and student loans. He originally borrowed money to pay for his education through a student loan program. He recently consolidated all of his student loans into one. The term of the loan is 10 years, and Benjamin is in his second year of payments. The current payment is $241.05 per month.

Credit Cards

Before marriage, Benjamin and Sarah each had their own credit cards, the balances of which are close to the maximum credit limits. After marriage, they applied for a joint credit card and planned to use it for emergencies only. The current interest rates, balances, limits, and annual fees on these cards are as follows.

	Interest Rate	Balance	Credit Limit	Annual Fee
Benjamin	18%	$4,750	$5,000	$50
Sarah	23%	$4,920	$5,000	$50
Joint	16%	$1,200	$5,000	$50

Bank Loans

During the past several years, Benjamin and Sarah have taken out loans to pay for vacations. The current payment is $604.27 per month. The balance of these loans is $9,909.

To assist the Reddings with their immediate cash flow needs, you offer to loan them $20,000 at an annual interest rate of 10%. You explain that such a loan would allow them to pay off almost all of their credit cards and bank loans at a significantly reduced interest rate. You tell them they can repay the loan in full, if they wish, when they receive the expected gifts of $10,000 each from Benjamin's Great Aunt Mabel.

Entertainment

Because of Benjamin and Sarah's hectic work schedules and the three children, they rarely get to spend time alone together. Every Friday night, they go to a moderately priced restaurant for dinner. Sometimes they are joined by some of Benjamin's colleagues, and he uses this time to network. The approximate cost of dinner each Friday for Benjamin and Sarah is $50 including a gratuity.

Friday nights are also a night out for the children. Delores brings the children to The Burger Barn for dinner. The approximate cost is $19 for all three children and Delores.

Education

Because of the quality of the schools in their state, Benjamin and Sarah want Scott, Janice, and Carly to go to private schools, but they are concerned about the cost. To assist in defraying the cost of educating the children, it is expected that all three children will attend Woodridge Preparatory School for K–12th grade. Sarah's position allows for tuition discounts (no additional multifamily discount) for teachers as follows:

- 50% discount on tuition for students in K–8th grades; and

- 75% discount on tuition for students in 9–12th grades.

Current tuition is $3,665 per student per year. Tuition is expected to increase at 5% per year. Each child will begin kindergarten at age 5.

Benjamin and Sarah would also like to provide financial assistance to their children while they attend college. They have decided to provide each child $15,000 (in today's dollars) per year for tuition, room, and board. Any additional funding will be provided by the trust, student loans, and part-time employment by the children. Today, tuition, fees, and other associated costs average $25,000 for a public university and are expected to increase at a rate of 5% per year. Each child is expected to begin college immediately after graduation from high school at age 18 and attend for four years.

QUESTIONS

1. List the Reddings' financial strengths and weaknesses.

2. After reading the case, what additional information would you request from the Reddings to complete your data-gathering phase?

3. Calculate the following financial ratios for the Reddings.

$$\frac{\text{Liquid Assets}}{\text{Monthly Expenses}}$$
$$\frac{\text{Net Worth}}{\text{Total Assets}}$$
$$\frac{\text{Total Debt}}{\text{Total Assets}}$$
$$\frac{\text{Total Debt}}{\text{Annual Total Income*}}$$
$$\frac{\text{Annual Housing and Debt Payments}}{\text{Annual Gross Income}}$$
$$\frac{\text{Annual Housing Costs}}{\text{Annual Gross Income}}$$
$$\frac{\text{Investment Assets}}{\text{Annual Gross Income}}$$
$$\frac{\text{Annual Savings}}{\text{Annual Gross Income}}$$
*Annual Total Income is the same as Annual Gross Income.

4. Comment on any of the above ratios that you think are important.

5. Briefly evaluate the Reddings' use of debt.

6. Assuming an earnings rate of 8%, calculate the amount needed today to fund the children's college education.

7. Assuming a rate of return of 8%, calculate the amount they need to save each month to fund the children's college education. Assume that savings will begin at the end of this month and continue until the youngest children begin college.

8. Assuming a rate of return of 8%, calculate the monthly savings needed for education assuming that savings will continue until the children's college education is completed.

9. Determine whether the Reddings will currently qualify to refinance their home. Is the house eligible for refinancing by a lender requiring a maximum loan-to-value ratio of 80%? How much cash would the Reddings need if they refinance?

10. Assuming that the Reddings decide to use their savings account to pay down the mortgage so they are able to refinance their current mortgage, calculate the monthly payment for each of the terms below. For purposes of this question, disregard whether the Reddings qualify to refinance their home. Assume they maintain the lender's loan-to-value ratio requirement.
    a. 15-year loan
    b. 30-year loan paid over 30 years
    c. 30-year loan paid over the remaining life of their current mortgage

11. Calculate the total expected savings from the refinancing for each of the three loans mentioned in Question 10.

12. Do they qualify for any of the loans in Question 10 if the bank requires a total housing cost ratio less than 28% and a total debt-to-payments income ratio of 36%?

13. If they do not qualify for any of the loans in Question 10 because the lender counts only $82,000 of income, what actions should they consider in order to qualify?

14. Calculate the total amount of money needed today to meet Julie's medical needs. Assume that she lives seven years and that the Reddings invest in corporate bonds.

15. How much do the Reddings need to save on a monthly basis beginning at the end of this month toward a down payment in order to purchase their future home for $300,000? Assume they invest at an interest rate equal to the expected return on the S&P 500 Index and pay all associated taxes out of their current budget.

16. Does the trust fund of $100,000 belong on the Reddings' Statement of Financial Position?

17. What are the deficiencies in the presentation of the Statement of Financial Position?

18. The Steiners decided to provide additional financial assistance to help with their grandchildren's college education expenses. They planned to elect gift-splitting for any gifts they made, and they wanted to give as much as they could without incurring any gift tax. What was the maximum amount they could have contributed in 2016 and still have met these objectives using Coverdell Education Savings Accounts (CESAs) and Section 529 plans?

ADDITIONAL QUESTIONS

1. What are the tax consequences of the current treatment of the tutoring income?

2. What, if any, are the tax consequences to the Reddings of the tuition discount the first year that all three children are in school?

3. What are the tax consequences that may result from the current treatment of the employment of Delores?

4. What are the Reddings' present insurance needs?

5. Discuss the Reddings' projected estate problems.

6. What estate planning recommendations would you make to the Reddings?

7. What tax planning recommendations would you make to the Reddings?

8. Estimate the adjusted gross income less itemized deductions for federal income tax for the Reddings for 2016.

9. Would it be beneficial for the Reddings to obtain a signed release from Delores indicating that she does not want withholding from payments made to her for child care services rendered?

10. If Sarah left Woodridge Preparatory School today, what would be her vested retirement balance?

11. How would Sarah's benefits be affected if her retirement plan was considered top heavy?

12. If Sarah left Woodridge Preparatory School today, what are her options regarding the balance in her retirement plan?

13. If the Reddings had a portfolio with the following asset allocation for retirement, what would be their expected return?

Aggressive stocks	10%
Growth stocks	10%
S&P 500 Index	40%
Corporate bonds	30%
Money market	10%
	100%

14. What is the weighted beta of the portfolio in Question 13?

15. Does the asset allocation in Question 13 match the Reddings' financial objectives and risk tolerance?

16. On the basis of the portfolio in Question 13, how much, in today's dollars, would the Reddings need to fund their retirement?

17. What is the approximate amount of life insurance that Benjamin needs to replace all of his income and raises during his work life expectancy assuming an investment rate of return equal to the rate of return associated with growth stocks?

18. Can the Reddings deduct the interest on the student loan for 2016 federal income tax purposes?

19. Discuss ways that Julie might use her life insurance policy to help meet the expenses associated with her terminal illness. Is a viatical agreement appropriate for her situation?

20. What was the maximum tax-deductible contribution Benjamin and Sarah could have made to traditional IRAs for 2016?

21. Delores frequently interacts with and watches over other children who are visiting the Reddings' children in the Reddings' home. Are Benjamin and Sarah adequately protected against a possible liability exposure if Delores negligently injures one of those children?

22. What are the tax consequences to Benjamin of the group term insurance policy?

23. Assume that Julie purchased a long-term care policy with a 5-year benefit period. The policy provides a daily benefit of $200 using a pool-of-money concept, with an elimination period of 60 days. The policy is tax-qualified (meets HIPAA requirements). The policy does not have an inflation rider.
    a. How can Julie qualify for the benefits under the policy?
    b. Assume Julie qualifies for long-term care benefits and enters a qualifying long-term care facility for a period of 7 years. She incurs costs for the entire 7-year period at today's rates. For how long will her policy provide benefits?

24. The Reddings' homeowners policy has an 80% coinsurance requirement which provides for reduced loss settlement if the Reddings carry less than 80% of the replacement cost value on their home. Assume the replacement cost of the Reddings' house is estimated by the insurance company to be $150,000. How much coverage should the Reddings purchase on the home for Coverage A-Dwelling?

25. Assuming the Reddings refinance their home and use the proceeds to retire debt, what is the tax consequence in the current tax year if one point is paid to secure the interest rate?

26. What ethical issues are raised by your offer to loan the Reddings $20,000 to pay off their credit cards and bank loans?

27. Assume the Reddings ask you to prepare their income tax return for the current year as part of your planning engagement with them. Despite your advice that they must report Sarah's tutoring income on their return and pay employment taxes on the money they pay to Delores, they remain unwilling to do so. They insist on omitting the tutoring income on their return and they refuse to file the necessary paperwork to report Delores's earnings. What are your ethical obligations in this scenario?

Nicholas and Whitney Clement

Today is January 1, 2017. Nicholas and Whitney Clement have come to you, a financial planner, for help in developing a plan to accomplish their financial goals. From your initial meeting together, you have gathered the following information.

Personal Background and Information

Nicholas Clement (Age 27)

Nicholas is an assistant in the marketing department for Energy Tech, Inc., a small company with 15 employees. His annual salary is $39,000.

Whitney Clement (Age 24)

Whitney is a legal research assistant with the law firm of Laurent, Heine & Merritt, LLC. Her annual salary is $30,000.

The Children

Nicholas and Whitney have no children from this marriage. Nicholas has two children, Grant, age 4, and Blake, age 3, from a former marriage. Grant and Blake live with their mother, Kelly.

The Clements

Nicholas and Whitney have been married for two years. Nicholas must pay $500 per month in child support until both Grant and Blake reach age 18. The divorce decree also required Nicholas to create an insurance trust for the benefit of the children and contribute $175 per month to the trust. The trustee is Kelly's father. The beneficiaries do not have withdrawal powers. The proceeds of the trust are to be used for the education and maintenance of the children in the event of Nicholas's death. The trustee has the power to invade any trust principal for the beneficiaries at the earlier of the death of Nicholas or Blake reaching age 18.

Personal and Financial Objectives

1. They would like to establish an emergency fund.

2. They want to eliminate debt.

3. They want to save for a 20% down payment on their first home. The current market value of the house is $150,000. Property taxes would be $1,800 annually, and the annual homeowners insurance premium would be $1,125.

4. They want to contribute to tax-advantaged savings plans.

5. They plan to have additional children in seven years.

6. They both plan to retire in 29 years.

Economic Information

- Inflation is expected to be 4% annually.

- Their salaries should increase 5% annually.

- They are not subject to a state income tax.

- The after-tax investment rate of return is 6%.

- Bank lending rates are as follows: 6% for a 15-year mortgage, 6.5% for a 30-year mortgage, and 8% for a secured personal loan.

Insurance Information

Life Insurance

	Policy A	Policy B	Policy C
Insured	Nicholas	Nicholas	Whitney
Face amount	$250,000	$117,000[2]	$30,000
Policy Type	Whole life	Group term	Group term
Cash value	$2,000	$0	$0
Annual premium	$2,100	$267	$75
Premium payor	Trustee	Employer	Employer
Beneficiary	Trust[1]	Kelly	Nicholas
Policyowner	Trust	Nicholas	Whitney

[1]Grant and Blake are equal beneficiaries of the trust.
[2]This was increased from $50,000 to $117,000 January 1, 2017.

Health Insurance

Nicholas and Whitney are covered under Nicholas's employer plan, which is a major medical plan with a $200 per person deductible, 80/20 coinsurance provision, and family annual stop loss limit of $1,500.

Long-Term Disability Insurance

Nicholas is covered by an own-occupation policy with premiums paid by his employer. The monthly benefit is equal to 60% of his gross pay after an elimination period of 180 days and is payable to age 65. The policy covers both sickness and accidents and is guaranteed renewable.

Whitney is not covered by disability insurance.

Renters Insurance

The Clements have a HO-4 renters policy without endorsements. Contents coverage: $25,000; liability limit: $100,000.

Automobile Insurance

Both car and truck*

Coverage Type	Policy Limits
Bodily injury	$25,000/$50,000
Property damage	$10,000
Medical payments	$5,000 per person
Uninsured motorist	$25,000/$50,000
Comprehensive deductible	$200
Collision deductible	$500
Premium (annual)	$4,950

*The Clements do not have any additional insurance on Whitney's motorcycle.

Investment Information

The Clements believe that they need six months of cash flow net of all taxes, savings, vacation, and net cash flow in an emergency fund. They are willing to include the savings account and Nicholas's Section 401(k) plan, because of the loan provision, in their emergency fund.

The Federal Express stock was a gift to Nicholas from his Uncle Frank. At the date of the gift (July 1, 2000), the fair market value of the stock was $3,500. Uncle Frank's tax basis was $2,500, and he paid gift tax of $1,400 on the gift.

The K&B stock of 100 shares was a gift to Whitney last Christmas from her Uncle Mike. At the date of the gift (December 25, 2016), the fair market value was $8,000, and Uncle Mike had paid $10,000 for the stock in 2004 (his tax basis).

The growth mutual fund (currently valued at $13,900) had been acquired by Nicholas over the years 2011, 2012, 2013, 2014, 2015, and 2016 with deposits of $1,000, $1,000, $2,000, $2,000, $2,500, and $3,000. The earnings were all reinvested and reported via Form 1099 each year:

Year	Reinvested Earnings
2011	$0
2012	$200
2013	$400
2014	$400
2015	$650
2016	$750

The growth mutual fund has a transfer-on-death (TOD) provision. The account is in Nicholas's name, and the beneficiary designation is Nicholas's mother. This provision was made prior to his marriage to Whitney.

Income Tax Information

The filing status of the Clements for federal income tax is married filing jointly. Both the children (Grant and Blake) are claimed as dependents on the Clements' tax return as part of the divorce agreement. Their marginal income tax rate is 15%, and FICA taxes are 7.65%. The Clements live in a state that does not have a state income tax.

Group Term Life Insurance Coverage Cost Per $1,000 of Protection For 1 Month	
Under age 25	$.05
Age 25 to 29	$.06

Retirement Information

Nicholas currently contributes 3% of his salary to his Section 401(k) plan. His employer matches $.50 for every dollar contributed up to a maximum of 3% of gross salary.

Gifts, Estates, Trusts, and Will Information

The Clements live in a common-law state that has adopted the Uniform Probate Code. Currently, Whitney does not have a will, while Nicholas has his will set up to leave his entire probate estate to his children.

STATEMENT OF CASH FLOWS
Nicholas and Whitney Clement
January 1, 2016 to December 31, 2016
(Expected to be similar in 2017)

CASH INFLOWS

Salaries

Nicholas—salary	$39,000	
Whitney—salary	30,000	
Investment income*	1,635	
Total inflows		$70,635

CASH OUTFLOWS

Savings—house down payment	$ 1,800	
Reinvestment of investment income	1,635	
Section 401(k) plan contribution	1,170	
Total savings		$ 4,605

FIXED OUTFLOWS

Child support	$ 6,000	
Life insurance payment (to trustee)	2,100	
Rent	9,900	
Renters insurance	720	
Utilities	1,080	
Telephone (home)	540	
Telephones (cell)	900	
Auto payment principal and interest	5,400	
Auto insurance	4,950	
Gas, oil, maintenance	3,600	
Student loans	3,600	
Credit card debt	4,500	
Furniture payments	1,952	
Total fixed outflows		$45,242

VARIABLE OUTFLOWS

Taxes—Nicholas FICA	$ 2,984	
Taxes—Whitney FICA	2,295	
Taxes—federal tax withheld	7,393	
Food	4,800	
Clothing	1,500	
Entertainment/vacation	1,920	
Total variable outflows		$20,892
Total cash outflows		$70,739
Net cash flow (deficit)		$ (104)

*$510 from dividends and $1,125 from other investment sources.

STATEMENT OF FINANCIAL POSITION
Nicholas and Whitney Clement
As of January 1, 2017

ASSETS[1]		LIABILITIES AND NET WORTH	
Cash and equivalents		**Liabilities[2]**	
Cash	$ 500	Credit card 1	$ 8,000
Savings account	1,000	Credit card 2	1,862
Total cash and equivalents	$ 1,500	Student loan—Nicholas[3]	45,061
		Auto loan—Whitney	21,179
Invested assets		Furniture loan	2,300
Federal Express stock (100 shares)[4]	$ 5,000	*Total liabilities*	$78,402
K&B stock (100 shares)	7,200		
Growth mutual fund	13,900		
Section 401(k) plan account	1,500	**Net worth**	($78)
Total invested assets	$27,600		
Use assets			
Auto—Whitney	$26,474		
Truck—Nicholas	4,000		
Motorcycle—Whitney	1,000		
Personal property and furniture	17,750		
Total use assets	$49,224		
Total assets	$78,324	**Total liabilities and net worth**	$78,324

Notes to Financial Statements
[1] Assets are stated at fair market value.
[2] Liabilities are stated at principal only as of January 1, 2017, before January payments.
[3] Nicholas's parents took out the student loans, but he is repaying them. Nicholas paid $2,732 in interest in 2016.
[4] Federal Express's current dividend is $3.40 per share.

Information Regarding Assets and Liabilities

Home Furnishings

The furniture was originally purchased with a 20% down payment and an 18% interest rate over 36 months. The monthly payment is $162.69.

Automobile

The automobile was purchased January 1, 2016, for $26,474 with 20% down and 80% financed over 60 months with payments of $450 per month.

Stereo System

The Clements have a high-end stereo system with a fair market value of $10,000. They asked and received permission to alter their apartment to build speakers into every room. The agreement with the landlord requires the Clements to leave the speakers if they move because the speakers are permanently installed and affixed to the property. The replacement value of the installed speakers is $4,500, and the non-installed components are valued at $5,500. The system was purchased with cash last year for $10,000.

QUESTIONS

1. What does *guaranteed renewable* mean with regard to Nicholas's disability policy?

2. What are the deficiencies in the Clements' disability insurance coverage?

3. How could the Clements cover their personal property for replacement value?

4. If the Clements were burglarized and had their movable stereo system components stolen, would they be covered under the HO-4 policy, and if so, for what value? (See Exhibit 9 in the Appendix for HO chart.)

5. If there was a fire in the Clements' apartment building and their in-wall speaker system was destroyed, would they be covered under the HO-4 policy, and if so, to what extent?

6. If a fire forced the Clements to move out of their apartment for a month, would the HO-4 policy provide any coverage?

7. Is Whitney covered for liability under the personal auto policy while driving her motorcycle?

8. Who will actually collect the proceeds of Nicholas's term life insurance if he were to die today, given that the Clements live in a Uniform Probate Code state?

9. How much must Nicholas's employer include in Nicholas's W-2 for 2016 for the group term life insurance? How much may be included in 2017?

10. Whitney sustained injuries while playing with Grant and Blake. Medical expenses totaled $1,600. The insurance company paid medical expenses in what amount? (Assume the Clements made no other medical claims this year prior to this claim.)

11. Using a human life value approach net of federal and state income taxes, how much additional life insurance is needed on Nicholas's life? (Round to the nearest $50,000 and assume that the marginal tax rate remains constant.)

12. Assume that Nicholas is in a serious automobile accident and is unable to perform the duties of his occupation for 208 consecutive days. What benefits will he receive under his long-term disability insurance policy? What will be the income tax consequences of receiving these benefits?

13. Assume that Nicholas is laid off from his job at Energy Tech, Inc. Typically, how many months of continuation health insurance coverage are the Clements entitled to under COBRA? If Nicholas and Whitney are divorced, how many months of continuation coverage is Whitney entitled to?

14. Assume Nicholas is driving his car on a foggy night and the car collides with a deer. As a result, Nicholas incurs medical expenses of $1,000, and his friend, Bill, who is riding with him, incurs medical expenses of $2,000. The front bumper of the car also sustains damage of $1,500. If Nicholas files a claim for these items under his personal auto policy (PAP), what amount will the policy pay?

15. Nicholas's son, Grant, is playing with a friend in the Clements' back yard. Both of them attempt a daring back flip off a picnic table and land on the ground injuring themselves. Each child sustains medical bills of $900 for emergency room x-rays. What coverage is provided under the homeowners policy for this incident?

ADDITIONAL QUESTIONS

1. List the Clements' financial strengths and weaknesses.

2. After reading the case, what additional information would you request from the Clements to complete your data-gathering phase?

3. Calculate the following financial ratios for the Clements.

$$\frac{\text{Liquid Assets}}{\text{Monthly Nondiscretionary Expenses}}$$

$$\frac{\text{Liquid Assets}}{\text{Current Debt Payments}}$$

$$\frac{\text{Net Worth}}{\text{Total Assets}}$$

$$\frac{\text{Total Debt}}{\text{Total Assets}}$$

$$\frac{\text{Total Debt}}{\text{Annual Gross Income}}$$

$$\frac{\text{Annual Housing and Debt Payments}}{\text{Annual Gross Income}}$$

$$\frac{\text{Annual Housing Costs}}{\text{Annual Gross Income}}$$

$$\frac{\text{Investment Assets}}{\text{Annual Gross Income}}$$

$$\frac{\text{Annual Savings}}{\text{Annual Gross Income}}$$

4. Comment on any of the above ratios that you think are important.

5. Describe the Clements' current financial condition.

6. If Nicholas and Whitney sell the K&B stock on January 1, 2017, for the fair market value shown on the statement of financial position, what are the income tax consequences?

7. Assuming that Nicholas and Whitney decide to sell the Federal Express stock on January 15, 2017, for a total price of $5,500, what are the tax consequences of such a sale?

8. As of January 1, 2017, how many payments have been made on the furniture?

9. Calculate the original purchase price of the furniture.

10. What is the approximate 2016 federal adjusted gross income (AGI) for the Clements?

11. How much more money must Nicholas and Whitney save to meet their emergency fund objective?

12. If the Clements sell the growth mutual fund for the Statement of Financial Position value, what will be the income tax consequences?

13. Assuming that the Clements are planning to buy their dream house seven years from now and expect housing costs to increase at the same rate as the general economic inflation rate, how much will they have to save at the end of each month to make the down payment if they plan to earn the assumed after-tax investment rate of return?

14. Do the payments of $175 a month to the trustee of the insurance trust for the children constitute a taxable gift?

15. Nicholas is considering borrowing from his Section 401(k) plan, which has a loan provision. What are the requirements for such a loan?

16. Nicholas and Whitney are contemplating contributing to individual retirement accounts (IRAs) for 2016 (by April 15, 2017). What do you advise them?

17. The Clements are trying to determine which is the better choice: the traditional IRA or the Roth IRA. Which do you recommend?

18. What is the implied growth rate of the Federal Express dividend based on the constant growth dividend discount model? Assume the Clements' required rate of return is 10%.

19. In the event of Nicholas's death, who would receive the growth mutual fund? Would the shares go through probate?

20. The Clements want to start improving their financial situation in anticipation of buying their dream house. What effect would it have on their net worth and cash flows if they liquidated enough of their invested assets to pay off their credit card debt and furniture loan?

21. How much federal income tax do the Clements owe on the $510 in dividends they received in 2016? Assume that all the dividends were received from stock in domestic corporations and that the Clements owned the stock for the entire year. The ex-dividend date was October 15.

22. Kelly is dissatisfied with the divorce decree and persuades the court to issue a new order stating that, in addition to the $175 monthly trust contribution, Nicholas must pay a total of $750 per month to Kelly until she remarries. The $400 portion of the monthly payment will terminate when Blake reaches age 18 whether or not Kelly remarries. The $750 payment under this new order replaces the former child support payments of $500. If Kelly dies before Blake reaches the age of 18, the new order states that only the $400 per month portion will be paid to the children until Blake reaches the age of 18, at which time all payments cease. What are the tax consequences of the new order to Kelly and Nicholas?

23. Nicholas and Whitney disclose in a meeting with you that they find woodworking relaxing. For the past five years, they have built and painted wooden Christmas lawn decorations on weekends in their backyard and have sold them to friends and family. The Clements have not been reporting income and expenses to the IRS. They incurred the following for the past five years:

Year	Income	Expenses
2012	$400	$450
2013	$375	$400
2014	$600	$500
2015	$750	$800
2016	$1,000	$600

They want to know how the income and expenses will be treated for tax purposes. What do you advise them?

24. Assume you recommend that the Clements purchase $300,000 of additional life insurance on Nicholas's life. The policy you recommend is a limited pay whole life policy with premiums payable for 20 years. You tell the Clements that the advantages of this policy are that it supplies the additional life insurance Nicholas needs and it will be fully paid up when Nicholas is 47 years old. The annual premium is $4,500. What ethical concern is raised by this recommendation?

25. Assume your brother-in-law sells investments in limited partnerships. His business is fairly new and you would like to help him get established. The limited partnership interests he sells are risky, but some of his investors have doubled their money in as little as 7 or 8 years. You are considering recommending that the Clements liquidate their $13,900 investment in the growth mutual fund and invest the proceeds with your brother-in-law. You feel that this may allow them to accumulate the money they need for a down payment on their first home fairly quickly. You feel there is no conflict of interest in making this recommendation because your brother-in-law pays you no compensation for referring clients to his firm. What potential ethical issues are raised in this scenario and what must you do to address them?

26. When the Clements reviewed their Statement of Cash Flows they were shocked at the cash flow deficit. The couple asks you what the impact of the new child support and alimony court order will have on their cash flows versus what you have already told them of its income tax effects. What do you tell the Clements?

7

Archie and Elaine Peyton

Today is January 1, 2017. Archie and Elaine Peyton have come to you, a financial planner, for help in developing a plan to accomplish their financial goals. From your initial meeting together, you have gathered the following information.

Personal Background and Information

Archie Peyton (Age 47)

Archie Peyton is an executive in ABC Company, a closely held corporation. His current salary is $100,000, and he expects increases of 5% per year.

Elaine Peyton (Age 50)

Elaine Peyton is Archie's administrative assistant. Her present salary is $24,000. She expects raises of 5% per year.

This is a second marriage for Elaine. Her first husband, Jerry, died five years ago. Elaine was the beneficiary of Jerry's $250,000 life insurance policy with which she created her investment portfolio.

The Peytons

Archie and Elaine have been married for three years. They do not reside in a community property state.

The Children

Elaine has two children from her first marriage, Jerry Jr., age 16, and Christopher, age 12. Archie and Elaine have one daughter, Kelsey, who is now 2 years old. All of the children live with them. The children are cared for during the day by their paternal grandmother who lives next door.

When they were first married, Archie wanted to adopt Jerry Jr. and Christopher, but the children refused. Since then, Archie and the two boys have been in continual conflict. As a result, Elaine expects to use her investment portfolio to pay for the boys' education, without any assistance from Archie.

Personal and Financial Objectives

1. The Peytons want to plan for their children's college education. They plan for each child to attend a private institution for five years beginning at age 18 with a cost of $25,000 a year per child (today's cost). The expected educational inflation rate is 6%.

2. Archie and Elaine expect to need 80% of their current pretax income during retirement. Elaine would like to retire at age 65 and Archie at age 62. They both expect their retirement period to be 30 years.

3. Archie wants to review both his and Elaine's life insurance needs and have estate planning documents drafted for both of them.

4. They would like to minimize any death tax liability.

5. Archie and Elaine plan to travel extensively during retirement.

6. They want to be debt free by the time they retire.

7. They want to pay off their credit card debt in the upcoming year.

Economic Information

■ Inflation has averaged 4% over the last 20 years.

■ Inflation is expected to be 3.5% for the foreseeable future.

(Assumed) Treasury Yield Curve

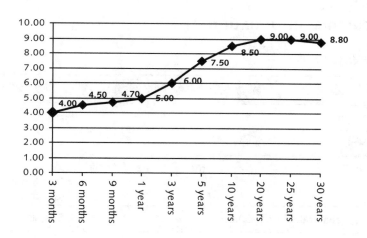

Current Yields for Treasury Securities

3 Months	6 Months	9 Months	1 Year	3 Years	5 Years	10 Years	20 Years	25 Years	30 Years
4.0%	4.5%	4.7%	5.0%	6.0%	7.5%	8.5%	9.0%	9.0%	8.8%

Current Mortgage Rates

- 8.75% for 30-year loans
- 8.25% for 15-year loans

Closing costs of 3% will not be included in the refinancing of the existing mortgage.

Economic Outlook—Investments

	Expected Returns (Pretax)	Expected Standard Deviation
Aggressive stocks	15%	15%
Growth stocks	12%	10%
S&P 500 Index	10%	8%
Corporate bonds	7%	3%
Money markets	5%	1%
90-day T-bills	4%	1%

Insurance Information

Life Insurance

	Policy A	Policy B	Policy C	Policy D
Insured	Archie	Archie	Elaine	Elaine
Owner	Archie	Archie	Elaine	Elaine
Beneficiary	Archie's mother	Estate of Archie	Jerry Jr. & Christopher (equally)	Jerry Jr. & Christopher (equally)
Original amount	$200,000	$100,000	$48,000	$50,000
Policy type	Group term	30-year decreasing term	Group term	Modified premium whole life
Cash value	$0	$0	$0	$0
Annual premium	$250	$100	$60	$420
Premium payor	Employer	Archie	Employer	Elaine
Date purchased	Annually	2008	Annually	2013
Current coverage	$200,000	$75,000	$48,000	$50,000

Health Insurance

The entire family is covered under the ABC Company health insurance plan. The Peytons currently pay $200 per month for the employer-provided major medical plan. The deductible is $500 per person up to a maximum of three persons. The policy contains a stop-loss limit of $5,000 per year and an 80/20 coinsurance provision.

Disability Insurance

Archie has a personally owned disability insurance policy that covers accident and sickness and has an own occupation definition with a 180-day elimination period. The policy pays monthly benefits of 60% of current gross income until Archie reaches age 65.

Homeowners Insurance

	HO-2 Policy
Dwelling	$150,000
Other structure	$ 15,000
Personal property*	$ 75,000
Loss of use (20% of dwelling)	$ 30,000

*No rider for replacement value on personal property. There is an endorsement for furs and jewelry (premium $30 annually).

Scheduled Personal Property Endorsement

This Endorsement Changes the Policy. Please Read Carefully.

For an additional premium, we cover the classes of personal property indicated by an amount of insurance. This coverage is subject to the DEFINITION, SECTION 1—CONDITIONS, SECTIONS I AND II—CONDITIONS and all provisions of this endorsement. The Section I deductible as shown on the Declarations does not apply to this coverage.

Class of Personal Property	Amount of Insurance	Premium
1. **Jewelry**, as scheduled.	$10,000	$30
2. **Furs** and garments trimmed with fur or consisting principally of fur, as scheduled.	Same as 1	
3. **Cameras**, projection machines, films, and related articles of equipment, as listed.	$5,000	$30
4. **Musical instruments** and related articles of equipment, as listed. You agree not to perform with these instruments for pay unless specifically provided under this policy.		
5. **Silverware**, silver-plated ware, goldware, gold-plated ware, and pewterware, but excluding pens, pencils, flasks, smoking implements, or jewelry.		
6. **Golfer's equipment** meaning golf clubs, golf clothing, and golf equipment.		
7. **Fine arts**, as scheduled. This premium is based on your statement that the property insured is located at the following address.		
8. **Postage stamps**		
9. **Rare and current coins**		

SCHEDULE*

Article	Description	Amount of Insurance
Diamond Bracelet	12 pure 1/3k diamonds, 14k white gold setting	$3,000
Diamond Necklace	18" 14k gold chain, pure 2k diamond pendant	$7,000
T-Max 90	35 mm body	$ 500
300Z lens		$3,000
Hasenbladt	camera body + 2 lens	$1,500

THE AMOUNTS SHOWN FOR EACH ITEM IN THE SCHEDULE ARE LIMITED BY CONDITION 2. LOSS SETTLEMENT ON PAGE 3 OF THIS ENDORSEMENT

* Entries may be left blank if shown elsewhere in this policy for this coverage

HO 04 61 04 91

Automobile Insurance

PERSONAL AUTO POLICY DECLARATIONS PAGE
COVERAGES

	Auto 1	Auto 2	Semiannual Premium
Part A—Liability	$100,000/$300,000	$100,000/$300,000	$400
Part B—Medical payments	$10,000	$10,000	$100
Part C—Uninsured motorists	$100,000/$300,000	$100,000/$300,000	$150
Part D—Damage to your auto			
Collision	$500 deductible	$500 deductible	$100
Other than collision	$250 deductible	$250 deductible	$ 70
Towing and labor	$100 maximum	$100 maximum	$ 10
Total semiannual premium			$830

Investment Information

During Elaine's marriage to Jerry, an education fund was established for both Jerry Jr. and Christopher. Since Jerry died, Elaine has no longer contributed to this fund. At the present time, the fund balance is $22,747. The money has been invested at 6%, and the Peytons have the option of renewing the short-term certificate of deposit (CD) in April at an interest rate of 4%.

When Elaine received the life insurance proceeds of $250,000 from Jerry's death, she asked a broker to help her manage the money. Her broker, John, placed her funds in an investment account over which he has full discretion. John's record regarding Elaine's investment portfolio over the last five years is as follows.

	2012	2013	2014	2015	2016
Load-adjusted total return	(10.0)	?	(8.5)	12.0	3.0

Elaine did not have the information for 2013 and has been unable to obtain it from John.

Elaine considers herself to be a conservative to moderate investor and has little experience or education in investments. Archie believes that he is a more moderate investor, and he has more experience with investments than Elaine.

Income Tax Information

The Peytons are in the 25% marginal tax bracket for federal income tax and 6% for state income tax.

Retirement Information

Both Elaine and Archie plan to retire when Elaine turns 65. They expect their retirement portfolio to earn a 10% pretax average annual rate of return. They also expect their retirement period to last 30 years. Social Security retirement benefits for Archie are expected to be $26,000 annually at age 67, while Elaine's Social Security benefit will be $9,600 annually at age 67.

Archie has not contributed to the traditional IRA in several years.

ABC Company sponsors a profit-sharing plan with a Section 401(k) feature. The Section 401(k) component of the plan allows participants to defer up to 20% of salary. The plan also matches $0.50 for every dollar contributed, up to 6% of salary. Neither Archie nor Elaine has ever made deferrals to the plan, but both have vested balances in the plan, as follows.

Vested Balance as of January 1, 2017	
Archie	$80,000
Elaine	$12,000

The plan allows participants to self-direct their retirement plan assets through the choice of various mutual funds.

ABC Company has recently established a phantom stock plan in which Archie is a participant. Archie's interest is 1% of ABC as of year-end 2016.

The investment options for the retirement plan are as follows.

XYZ Small Company Growth Fund	
Fund objective:	The Fund seeks long-term growth of capital.
Portfolio concept:	The Fund invests primarily in common stock of small-and medium-size companies that are early in their life cycle and have the potential to become major enterprises.

XYZ Growth Fund	
Fund objective:	The Fund seeks growth of capital and, secondarily, income.
Portfolio concept:	The Fund seeks to invest in equity securities (stocks) placing primary emphasis on those securities that Fund Management believes to be undervalued. The Fund may invest up to 20% in foreign securities.

XYZ Index Fund	
Fund objective:	The Fund seeks to approximate the total return of the S&P 500 Index.
Portfolio concept:	The Fund invests primarily in a portfolio of equity securities (stocks) that are included in the S&P 500 Index.

XYZ Foreign Fund	
Fund objective:	The Fund seeks long-term capital growth through investments in stocks and debt obligations of companies and governments outside the United States.
Portfolio concept:	The Fund generally invests in common stocks; however, it may also invest in preferred stocks and certain debt securities, rated or unrated, such as convertible bonds and bonds selling at a discount.

XYZ Balanced Fund	
Fund objective:	The Fund seeks the highest total investment return consistent with prudent risk.
Portfolio concept:	The Fund has a fully managed investment policy utilizing equity, debt, and convertible securities.

XYZ Income Fund	
Fund objective:	The Fund seeks a high level of income, consistent with the prudent investment of capital, through a flexible investment program emphasizing high-grade bonds.
Portfolio concept:	The Fund invests primarily in a broad range of high-grade, income-producing securities, such as corporate bonds and government securities.

XYZ Money Market Fund	
Fund objective:	The Fund seeks preservation of capital, current income, and liquidity.
Portfolio concept:	The Fund is a money market mutual fund that seeks capital preservation, current income, and liquidity through investment in a portfolio of high-quality, short-term money market instruments, including securities is issued by the U.S. government, its agencies, or instrumentalities.

The company has made the following profit-sharing contributions to the retirement plan for Archie and Elaine for each of the related years.

	Archie	Elaine
2017	None	None
2016	$15,000	$3,600
2015	$ 0	$ 0
2014	$13,605	$3,265
2013	$10,366	$2,488
2012	$ 8,954	$2,369
Balance 1/1/12	$25,000	$ 0

All contributions are made December 31 of the indicated year.

ANNUALIZED RETURNS OF RETIREMENT FUNDS

	2006	2007	2008	2009	2010	2011	2012	2013	2014	2015	2016
XYZ Small Co. Growth Fund	—	—	—	—	—	—	—	—	4.83%	41.14%	15.01%
XYZ Growth Fund	—	—	—	32.96%	0.03%	25.20%	9.97%	32.37%	1.77%	36.82%	14.50%
XYZ Index Trust	—	—	—	—	—	—	—	9.66%	1.02%	37.23%	13.25%
XYZ Foreign Fund	28.77%	24.75%	21.99%	30.53%	–3.01%	18.25%	0.10%	36.82%	0.35%	11.15%	7.08%
XYZ Balanced Fund	19.89%	4.60%	17.04%	22.98%	1.08%	24.69%	5.03%	13.71%	0.91%	32.87%	11.60%
XYZ Income Fund	14.75%	0.74%	8.91%	12.75%	8.32%	17.32%	6.74%	12.58%	–4.43%	18.54%	9.21%
XYZ Money Market Fund	4.21%	3.87%	4.01%	5.02%	5.40%	4.75%	5.00%	5.25%	6.01%	6.71%	5.20%

Gifts, Estates, Trusts, and Will Information

They do not have any estate planning documents at this time.

STATEMENT OF CASH FLOWS
Archie and Elaine Peyton
For January 1, 2016 to December 31, 2016
(Projected to be similar for 2017)

CASH INFLOWS

Salaries

Archie	$100,000	
Elaine	24,000	
Total salaries	$124,000	

Investment income

ML Brokerage Account	$ 3,050	
Elaine's investment portfolio	4,771	
Savings account	618	
Elaine's education fund	1,062	
Investment income	$ 9,501	
Total cash inflows		**$133,501**

CASH OUTFLOWS

Living expenses

Food	$ 4,300	
Clothing	4,000	
Entertainment	6,500	
Utilities, cable, and phone	5,000	
Auto maintenance	1,200	
Church	2,000	
Home mortgage	14,934	
Auto loans	18,818	
Credit card	4,300	
Total living expenses	$ 61,052	

Insurance

Health	$ 2,400	
Auto	1,660	
Life	520	
Homeowners with endorsements	950	
Disability	1,677	
Total insurance	$ 7,207	

Taxes

Property (residence)	$ 4,452	
Federal income (withholdings)	36,840	
State income	4,000	
Payroll (FICA) (Schedule 1)	9,486	
Total taxes	$ 54,778	

Total cash outflows		**$123,037**
Net cash flow (surplus)		**$10,464**

Schedule 1: Payroll Taxes

Old-Age, Survivors, and Disability Insurance

Archie	$100,000 × 6.2%	=	$6,200
Elaine	$ 24,000 × 6.2%	=	$1,488
			$7,688

Medicare

Archie	$100,000 × 1.45%	=	$1,450
Elaine	$ 24,000 × 1.45%	=	$ 348
			$1,798
Total			**$9,486**

2016 Payroll Tax Limits		
	Income	Tax Rate
OASDI	$118,500	6.2%
Medicare	Unlimited	1.45%

STATEMENT OF FINANCIAL POSITION
Archie and Elaine Peyton
As of January 1, 2017

Assets[1]			Liabilities[2] and Net Worth		
Liquid assets			**Short-term liabilities**		
JT	Checking[3]	$ 7,500	S2	Credit cards	$ 4,300
JT	Savings[4]	15,450			
	Total liquid assets	$ 22,950		**Long-term liabilities**	
	Invested assets		JT	Home mortgage	$144,981
S1	First Mutual Growth Fund[5]	$ 7,950	S1/S2	Auto loans	40,069
S1	ML Brokerage Account[6]	100,000	S1	Margin loan[7]	7,500
S2	Elaine's investment portfolio	210,000		**Total long-term**	$192,550
S2	Elaine's education fund	22,747			
S1	Archie's vested retirement plan account	80,000		**Total liabilities**	$196,850
S2	Elaine's vested retirement plan account	12,000			
S1	Archie's individual retirement account (IRA)[8]	9,000			
	Total invested assets	$441,697			
	Use assets				
JT	Home	$185,000		**Net worth**	$552,797
S1	Truck	32,000			
S2	Car	21,000			
S1	Boat	10,000			
S2	Furs and jewelry	10,000			
JT	Furniture and household	27,000			
	Total use assets	$285,000		**Total liabilities**	
	Total assets	$749,647		**and net worth**	$749,647

Notes to financial statements
[1]All assets are stated at fair market value.
[2]Liabilities are stated at principal only.
[3]The checking account is a noninterest-bearing account.
[4]The savings account earns 4% per year.
[5]See detail of fund.
[6]ML Brokerage Account is stated at gross value, which does not include margin loan of $7,500.
[7]Margin loan is for ML Brokerage Account. Interest rate is currently 8%.
[8]Archie's IRA is currently invested in CDs at a local bank.

Title designations
  S1 = Archie's property
  S2 = Elaine's property
  JT = Joint tenancy with right of survivorship

Information Regarding Assets and Liabilities

Investment Income

ML Brokerage Account	
Money market	$ 300
Bonds	3,350
Margin interest	(600)
	$3,050
Elaine's investment portfolio	
Bonds	$1,300
Stocks	3,471
	$4,771
Savings account	$ 618
Elaine's education fund	$1,062
TOTAL	**$9,501**

House

Principal residence	January 1, 2014 (purchase)
Fair market value (current)	$185,000
Original loan	$148,000
Term	30 years
Interest rate	9.5%
Monthly payment	$1,244.46
Remaining mortgage	$144,981
Remaining term	27 years

Boat

The boat is a 90-horsepower fishing boat that was originally bought for $10,000 and is owned outright.

Automobiles

	Archie's 2015 Truck	Elaine's 2014 Car
Purchase price	$40,000	$35,000
Down payment	$0	$10,000
Term	48 months	48 months
Interest rate	7%	8%
Monthly payment	$957.85	$610.32
Payments remaining	33	20
Outstanding balance	$28,677.07	$11,392.23

ML Brokerage Account

Account Name: Archie Peyton
Account Number: AB100402

Balances

Money Market	Price/share	Shares	Current Yield	Fair Market Value
Money market	$ 1.00	6,667.00	4.5%	$6,667.00

Bonds	Maturity	Coupon	Cost Basis	Fair Market Value
$10,000 U.S. Treasury note	5	7.5%	$10,351.18	$10,000.00
$15,000 U.S. Treasury bond	25	6.0%	13,138.64	10,579.83
$50,000 U.S. Treasury bond	30	0.0%	4,093.40	3,982.02
$20,000 Davidson debenture	20	8.5%	17,455.93	16,288.44
			$45,039.15	$40,850.29

Stocks	Price/share	Shares	Cost Basis	Fair Market Value
Stock 1*	$ 5.20	2,000	$10,000	$10,400
Stock 2*	$ 4.85	1,500	6,750	7,275
Stock 3*	$26.00	500	11,250	13,000
			$28,000	$30,675

* These stocks do not currently pay dividends.

Mutual Funds	Price/share	Shares	Cost Basis	Fair Market Value
Emerging growth fund	$21.00	500	$12,250	$10,500
Balanced fund	$18.00	425	8,925	7,650
Municipal bond fund	$12.00	250	3,500	3,000
			$24,675	$21,150

Note: All distributions from these funds are reinvested.

Options	Number of Options Contracts	Option Premium	Exercise Price	Option Expiration	Fair Market Value
Stock 2 call options	5	$3.00	$ 5.50	July 2017	$486.37
Stock 3 put options	5	$5.00	$24.00	March 2017	$171.34
					$657.71

TOTAL ACCOUNT VALUE	**$100,000**
MARGIN LOAN BALANCE	**$7,500**
NET ACCOUNT VALUE	**$92,500**

First Mutual Growth Fund

Account Name: Archie Peyton
Account Number: AB100357

Transaction	Date	Amount	Price/Share	Shares	Total Shares	Total Value
Buy	04/01/15	$ 2,500	$25.00	100	100	$ 2,500
Buy	08/01/15	$ 4,000	$20.00	200	300	$ 6,000
Reinvest dividend	12/01/15	$ 500	$12.50	40	340	$ 4,250
Buy	02/01/16	$ 3,000	$15.00	200	540	$ 8,100
Buy	04/01/16	$ 2,000	$20.00	100	640	$12,800
Buy	06/01/16	$ 1,500	$25.00	60	700	$17,500
Sell	12/01/16	$11,880	$27.00	(440)	260	$ 7,020
Reinvest dividend	12/01/16	$ 1,080	$27.00	40	300	$ 8,100
BALANCE	12/31/16	—	$26.50	—	300	$ 7,950

Note: All distributions from this fund are reinvested.

Elaine's Investment Portfolio

Bonds

Bonds	Term	Duration	Current Fair Market Value
$10,000 U.S. Treasury bonds	10	7.12 years	$10,000
$5,000 U.S. Treasury bonds	20	9.95 years	$ 5,000
		Total value of bonds	$15,000

Stocks

Shares	Stock	$\bar{X}$	Beta	σ	R^2	P/E Ratio	Dividend Yield	Basis	Fair Market Value
1,000	Stock A	6%	0.65	11%	75%	13.0	3.0%	$30,000	$ 38,000
575	Stock B	11%	0.75	9%	65%	14.0	3.7%	$45,000	$ 46,000
200	Stock C	7%	0.65	10%	30%	15.1	3.7%	$20,000	$ 17,000
500	Stock D	3%	0.70	8%	45%	25.2	0.0%	$11,000	$ 8,500
1,000	Stock E	25%	0.95	15%	70%	14.4	0.0%	$20,000	$ 18,000
1,250	Stock F	22%	1.10	18%	20%	11.1	0.0%	$23,000	$ 25,000
							Total value of stocks		$152,500

Mutual Funds

Shares	Mutual Fund	Style	$\bar{X}$	Alpha	Beta	σ	R^2	Front-End Load	Expense Ratio	Basis	Fair Market Value
210	Fund A	MG	14%	3%	1.1	12%	57%	4.5%	.71%	$ 2,500	$ 2,625
300	Fund B	LG	11.5%	.5%	0.94	8%	81%	4.5%	1.0%	$ 5,000	$ 5,100
443	Fund C	MV	6%	(4%)	0.65	8%	42%	4.5%	2.25%	$10,000	$11,075
1,000	Fund D	MG	−6%	(10%)	0.70	20%	4%	4%	1.85%	$ 8,000	$ 7,500
320	Fund E	LG	4%	(3%)	1.1	5%	60%	0%	1.75%	$ 9,500	$ 8,000
410	Fund F	LG	7%	(2.5%)	0.9	3%	78%	3%	1.5%	$10,000	$ 8,200
									Total value of mutual funds		$42,500

Note: All distributions from the mutual funds are reinvested.

TOTAL PORTFOLIO VALUE   **$210,000**

Key	
$\bar{X}$	5-year average return
σ	Standard deviation
R^2	Coefficient of determination
L	Large
M	Medium
G	Growth
V	Value

QUESTIONS

1. As of December 1, 2016, what is the internal rate of return for the First Mutual Growth Fund since the Peytons' first purchase on April 1, 2015?

2. How does a change in the price of the below-listed stocks affect the profit/loss of the related option? Each change (A–D) is independent.

ML Brokerage Account

	Stock	Price Changes To
Change A	Stock 2	$6.00
Change B	Stock 2	$4.00
Change C	Stock 3	$29.00
Change D	Stock 3	$20.00

3. Calculate the geometric mean return since inception for each of the funds in the ABC Company retirement plan.

4. Determine the Sharpe and Treynor ratios for each mutual fund in Elaine's investment portfolio. Assume a risk-free rate equal to the 90-day T-bill rate.

5. Rank each of the funds in Elaine's investment portfolio by the Sharpe and Treynor ratios. Comment on the results and the meaning of the numbers.

6. What is the coupon rate for each of the two bonds in Elaine's portfolio?

7. Comment on the allocation of mutual funds in Elaine's portfolio.

8. Comment on Elaine's broker's choice of mutual funds in her portfolio.

9. How have ABC Company's contributions to retirement plan accounts for Archie and Elaine performed since January 1, 2012?

10. If the Peytons had earned an average return equal to that of the XYZ Balanced Fund (calculated in Question 3) on the ABC Company's profit-sharing plan contributions to the Peytons' plan accounts, how much better off would they be?

11. What is the expected market value of the following bonds in the ML Brokerage Account if interest rates decrease by 1%? Assume interest is paid semiannually.
    - $10,000 U.S. Treasury note
    - $15,000 U.S. Treasury bond
    - $50,000 U.S. Treasury bond

12. Is the current yield curve consistent with the Liquidity Preference Theory? Why or why not?

13. Is the current yield curve consistent with the Market Segmentation Theory? Why or why not?

14. What was the rate of return on Elaine's investment portfolio in 2013?

15. If the interest rates for all maturities increase by 1%, what will be the approximate value of the bonds in Elaine's investment portfolio?

16. What is the total percentage and dollar investment gain related to Stock 2 that Archie would realize if the price of Stock 2 increases to $7.50 upon option expiry (in Brokerage Account)?

17. Has Archie done an effective job of immunizing Stock 3 from downside risk? Why or why not?

18. What is the weighted duration of the bond portfolio portion of Elaine's investment portfolio?

19. What is the holding period return (HPR) for Elaine's stock portfolio portion held in her investment portfolio?

20. What is the weighted beta of Elaine's mutual funds located in her investment portfolio?

ADDITIONAL QUESTIONS

1. List the Peytons' financial strengths and weaknesses.

2. After reading the case, what additional information would you request from the Peytons to complete your data-gathering phase?

3. Calculate the following financial ratios for the Peytons.

$\dfrac{\text{Liquid Assets}}{\text{Monthly Expenses}}$
$\dfrac{\text{Liquid Assets}}{\text{Current Monthly Debt Payments}}$
$\dfrac{\text{Net Worth}}{\text{Total Assets}}$
$\dfrac{\text{Total Debt}}{\text{Total Assets}}$
$\dfrac{\text{Total Debt}}{\text{Annual Total Income*}}$
$\dfrac{\text{Housing (PITI)**}}{\text{Monthly Gross Income}}$
$\dfrac{\text{Housing and Monthly Debt Payments}}{\text{Monthly Gross Income}}$
$\dfrac{\text{Investment Assets}}{\text{Annual Gross Income*}}$
* Annual total income is the same as annual gross income.   ** PITI: principal, interest, taxes, and insurance.

4. Comment on any of the above ratios that you think are important to their financial plan.

5. What is the taxable gain on the sale of the 440 shares of First Mutual Growth Fund (December 1, 2016), and how will it be classified for income tax purposes? Assume that the tax basis in the shares sold is determined by using the first in, first out (FIFO) method.

6. What are the other two methods of determining the tax basis of the 440 shares of First Mutual Growth Fund sold on December 1, 2016?

7. As of January 1, 2017, what is the average cost per share for the shares remaining of First Mutual Growth Fund, assuming the FIFO method was used for determining the sale of the 440 shares?

8. For a HO-2 policy, what type of coverage is provided by loss of use?

9. Elaine has decided that the education fund and her investment account will be used for funding the cost of college for the boys. Elaine wants to set aside enough of these assets to fund their education with the remainder being used to fund Kelsey's college education. Ignoring the transaction costs of selling the current assets, how much does she need to set aside for the boys' college education if she wants to invest in an even mix of 5-year and 10-year Treasury bonds? Assume all taxes will be paid out of current income.

10. Elaine wants to know how much she and Archie need to contribute over the next 15 years for Kelsey's education. Their first contribution will be in one year, and they will invest in a portfolio that is split equally between the S&P 500 and 5-year Treasury bonds. This allocation will be maintained by rebalancing the account every six months. Assume the tax on earnings will be paid from their income.

11. **a.** If Archie were to become disabled on May 30, 2017, when would he collect benefits and how much would he receive during 2017?
    b. What are the tax consequences of receiving disability benefits?

12. How much of their current gross income, in dollars and percentages, are the Peytons currently saving toward their retirement goal?

13. Ignoring Social Security benefits, how much money should the Peytons have accumulated using a capital needs analysis and the following approaches?

    a. The annuity approach.

    b. The capital preservation approach.

    c. The purchasing power preservation approach.

14. What do the Peytons need to do now to meet their retirement income goal? They do not want to consider Social Security benefits in their retirement planning.

15. Could the Peytons benefit from itemizing deductions on their 2016 income tax return? If so, what type of interest deductions can they take?

16. Discuss the Peytons' current life insurance situation.

17. Calculate the value of Archie's probate assets were he to die today. Assume that Elaine is the designated beneficiary of his IRA.

18. What are their current estate planning deficiencies?

19. Do they qualify for refinancing their home mortgage?

20. Calculate the payments and savings from the alternative ways to refinance.

21. What would be their payments if the Peytons kept their current mortgage and amortized it over the next 15 years?

22. Assuming Archie bought the balanced fund in 2013, what would be the income tax consequence for him by selling all the shares in 2016 using the average cost basis method? What is his loss/gain per share on the sale? What is his total loss/gain on the sale of the fund?

23. Elaine Peyton was recently in a car accident with the Smith family, in which she was found to be at fault, and has provided her automobile insurance company with the following bills:

    $12,000 damage to the Smiths' vehicle—actual cash value

    $7,500 damage to Elaine's vehicle—actual cash value

    $15,000 medical bills for Elaine

    $125,000 medical bills for the Smiths (Mr. Smith: $75,000; Mrs. Smith: $50,000)

    Based on the information provided, what would be the total amount of coverage provided by the Peytons' automobile policy?

24. Discuss the Peytons' homeowners and personal property coverage, including the boat.

25. Assume that one afternoon the Peytons call you and tell you they are taking their planning business to a firm that Elaine's broker, John, has recommended to them. They say John has told them that the firm he recommends will charge a lower fee and deliver a higher quality of service. They also ask you to return their personal documents and files immediately so they can begin working with the other firm. You tell the Peytons you will return their documents and files as soon as they pay you in full for the services you have already provided and you have a chance to talk to John. After speaking with the Peytons, you call John to complain about his actions. A heated argument ensues, and at one point you threaten to file a complaint against John's firm with CFP Board. What ethical concerns are raised by this scenario?

26. Assume Elaine brings several pieces of her jewelry to your office and asks you to secure an appraisal of them for insurance purposes. You assign the task of securing the appraisal to an intern in your office and give the jewelry to her, along with some jewelry belonging to another client who also wants an appraisal. Unbeknownst to you, the intern takes the jewelry home, intending to secure the appraisal first thing in the morning. That evening, she wears a set of Elaine's earrings and a necklace belonging to another client to a party. In the morning, she takes the jewelry to a jeweler for an appraisal and then returns the pieces to your office. What professional conduct issues are raised by this scenario, and what should you have done to prevent these issues from occurring?

27. After the results of the Peytons' retirement needs calculation showed the couple was not currently on target to meet their retirement income savings goal, they ask you how much more they should save in order to meet the retirement need and also have enough retirement savings to meet their goal of traveling extensively during retirement. What do you do next to answer the couple's question?

Clara Morrish

Today is January 1, 2017. Clara Morrish has come to you, a financial planner, for help in developing a plan to accomplish her financial goals. From your initial meeting together, you have gathered the following information.

Personal Background and Information

Clara Morrish (Age 69)

Clara is a retired homemaker. She is a recent widow. Clara's 70th birthday will be April 1, 2017.

Tim Morrish (deceased)

Clara was married to Tim Morrish, who died November 1, 2016, at the age of 69, after a brief battle with cancer. His date of birth was June 1, 1947.

Tim's estate is in probate. Tim was employed 45 years as a supervisor at ABC Co., Inc. (ABC) before retiring at age 65.

The Morrishes

They were married for 50 years. Clara's health is fair.

The Morrishes' Children

Clara has two children from her marriage to Tim: George (age 50) and Vince (age 49). George and Vince are each married, healthy, employed, and self-sufficient.

The Morrishes' Grandchildren

George and his wife, Kathy, have one daughter, Sarah (age 18). Sarah is currently a senior in high school and will be a freshman at a university in September. The cost of tuition for the university is currently $20,000. Clara would like to pay Sarah's tuition for this year. As a graduation gift, Clara is paying for Sarah's trip to Europe this summer. The cost of this trip is $3,000.

Vince and his wife, Laena, have one son, Kirby (age 17). Kirby is a junior in high school. Kirby is in need of orthodontic work that will cost $6,000. Clara would like to pay for Kirby's orthodontic work. Clara is also considering gifting stock worth $9,000 to Kirby.

Personal and Financial Objectives

1. Clara wants to have sufficient income at retirement ($30,000 per year in today's dollars including Social Security benefits).

2. Clara will consider acquiring a smaller residence.

3. Clara wants to explore long-term care alternatives (average annual cost in today's dollars $40,000).

4. Clara wants to donate to the American Cancer Society.

5. Clara wants to provide for her children and grandchildren.

6. Clara wants to pay Sarah's university tuition ($20,000).

7. Clara wants to gift stock to Kirby ($9,000).

8. Clara wants to pay for Kirby's orthodontic work ($6,000).

9. Clara wants to send Sarah to Europe ($3,000).

Economic Information

■ Inflation is expected to be 4% annually.

■ She lives in a state with no state income tax.

■ Stocks are expected to grow at 9.5%.

■ Bank lending rates are as follows: 6.5% for a 15-year mortgage, 7.5% for a 30-year mortgage, and 10% for a secured personal loan.

Life Expectancies from Table III, Uniform Lifetime

Age	Life Expectancy Factor
70	27.4
71	26.5
72	25.6

Insurance Information

Life Insurance
Irrevocable Life Insurance Trust (ILIT)

Tim created an ILIT 10 years ago. The only assets in the trust are $200,000 in proceeds from the life insurance policy the ILIT owned at Tim's death. The income beneficiary of the ILIT is Clara. The remainder beneficiaries are the grandchildren. Clara currently receives an annual income of $10,000 based on a return of 5% on the trust assets.

Health Insurance

Tim and Clara were both covered under Medicare Part A and B until the time of his death. Clara is still covered under Medicare Part A and B.

Investment Information

Clara's investment risk tolerance is low.

Income Tax Information

The Morrishes filed as married filing jointly for 2015. Clara and Tim have always lived in a community property state.

Clara has been making and selling jewelry for six years with some success. Since Tim's death last year, she has devoted more time to her craft and enjoys it tremendously. Her grandson, Kirby, created a website for her last year and Clara is amazed at the sales results. While she had been traveling to jewelry shows for most of her sales, the online sales this year have eliminated the need to travel. Because Clara will be itemizing her deductions this year, she believes she can report her income and expenses on Schedule C. Her gross sales from the jewelry business this year are $19,500. Her expenses in 2016 were:

Cost of goods sold	$12,900
Supplies	$ 500
Web-related costs	$ 600
Web advertising	$ 200
Postage/delivery costs	$ 1,200

She has kept detailed records from the beginning and can track her profit and loss from each year. In Year 1 she had a loss of $2,000; Year 2 was a loss of $1,000; Year 3 showed a profit of $3,000; Year 4 had another loss of only $500; Year 5 showed a profit of $6,000.

Retirement Information

Tim had a profit-sharing plan sponsored by ABC with Clara designated as the beneficiary. The plan has a value of $150,000 as of January 1, 2017. The plan permits the beneficiary to take a lump-sum distribution.

Clara currently has an IRA with Tim as the named beneficiary. Clara is the named beneficiary on Tim's IRA. They had both decided to defer IRA withdrawals until they are mandatory after age 70½. Clara has no plans to change this since Tim's death. She will rollover Tim's IRA into an inherited IRA in her name early in 2017. Both Tim and Clara began receiving Social Security benefits on their 65th birthdays. Tim's benefit for 2017 would have been $1,200 per month, and Clara's benefit for 2017 was estimated to be $600 per month.

Gifts, Estates, Trusts, and Will Information

Tim's will left all probate assets to Clara. The grandchildren are named as contingent beneficiaries (equally). Clara does not have a will.

STATEMENT OF FINANCIAL POSITION
Tim (deceased) and Clara Morrish
As of January 1, 2017

Assets[1]			Liabilities and Net Worth		
Cash and equivalents			**Liabilities[2]**		
CP	Cash	$ 25,000	Credit cards[3]		$ 20,000
CP	Savings account	20,000			
	Total cash and equivalents	$ 45,000			
Invested assets					
S1	Stocks[6]	$ 20,000	*Total liabilities*		$ 20,000
CP	IRA - Clara's	40,000			
CP	IRA - Tim's	50,000			
CP	Profit-sharing plan[7]	150,000	**Net worth**		$ 980,000
	Total invested assets	$ 260,000			
Personal use assets					
CP	Primary Residence[4]	$ 400,000			
S2	Vacation Home[5]	200,000			
CP	Auto	18,000			
CP	Furniture and personal property	77,000			
	Total use assets	$ 695,000			
Total assets		$1,000,000	**Total liabilities and net worth**		$1,000,000

Notes to financial statements
[1]Assets are stated at fair market value.
[2]Liabilities are stated at principal only as of January 1, 2017, before January payments. All liabilities are community property.
[3]Interest rate 18.3%.
[4]The primary residence was originally purchased for $110,000. There have been no additions or upgrades. The FMV was $400,000 on Tim's date of death.
[5]The vacation home was inherited by Clara from her mother. Adjusted tax basis is $125,000.
[6]Inherited from a sibling.
[7]Present value of Tim's profit-sharing plan

Other notes to financial statements
The income beneficiary of the ILIT is Clara. Remainder beneficiaries are the grandchildren. The ILIT is not listed on the Statement of Financial Position.

Title designations:
S1 - Tim
S2 - Clara
CP - Community property

Information Regarding Assets and Liabilities

Primary Residence

- Purchased April 1, 1981
- Market value $400,000 as of November 1, 2016, and January 1, 2017
- Original purchase price $110,000

Vacation Home

- This home is owned by Clara (fee simple).
- Clara inherited the home from her mother who paid $75,000 for it. The fair market value at the date of transfer to Clara was $125,000 in July 2000.
- The current fair market value is $200,000.
- The vacation home is located in a noncommunity property state. All payments for repairs and maintenance have been made by using community property assets.

QUESTIONS

1. What is Clara's federal income tax filing status for 2016, 2017, 2018, and 2019?

2. On November 1, 2017, Clara decides to sell her personal residence for the fair market value as of January 1, 2017. What will be her tax consequences? Disregard the vacation home.

3. Clara will attain age 70½ in 2017. If she elects to take a distribution from Tim's profit-sharing plan in 2017, to what extent will she be required to include it in her gross income?

4. How should Clara report the income and expenses from her jewelry business for 2016?

5. Ten years ago, Tim and Clara gave their grandchildren stock in a U.S. domestic corporation that is publicly traded. Because of an important advance in technology in the last year, the company is growing rapidly and in 2017 it pays $2,200 in qualified dividends to each child. What are the kiddie tax implications of the dividends on the income of the grandchildren in 2017? To their parents (assume a marginal tax rate of 25%)? To Clara?

6. Rather than let the vacation home sit unused during Tim's last illness, Tim and Clara rented it to vacationers for 180 days in 2016. However, Clara used her vacation home for the last 40 days of the year after Tim's death in 2016. The only expenses for the home were utilities, taxes, and maintenance. How much of these expenses may she deduct? Where does she report the income and expenses on her tax return in 2016?

7. How much of Tim's IRA must Clara include in taxable income in 2016?

8. How much of Clara's Social Security is taxable in 2017?

9. What is Clara's gross income in 2017?

10. Assume that in 2018, Clara decides to sell the stock she inherited from Tim that now has a fair market value of $24,000. She directs the broker to make the check payable to her sons, George and Vince, because she does not need the extra income from the sale. What are the tax consequences to Clara, George, and Vince as a result of this stock sale in the year of the sale?

11. A thief entered Clara's home on New Year's Day in 2017 while she was away from home and stole an antique gun that had been one of Tim's treasures that he had purchased for $3,500. Unfortunately, while Clara had the gun appraised after Tim's death, she did not specifically insure it and only recovered $200 for the gun that had been valued at $4,500. Assuming her AGI is the same in 2017 as in 2016, how much may Clara claim as a casualty loss on her tax return for 2017?

12. Assume that Clara's best friend, Marlene, who is 67 and legally blind, is in poor health and has only a meager Social Security income of $3,250 annually. Clara invited her to live with her beginning January 1, 2017, and is providing more than 50% of her total support. Assuming her AGI is the same in 2017 as in 2016, how will this affect Clara's personal and dependency exemptions in 2017?

13. Sarah, Clara's granddaughter, has a qualified tuition plan (QTP) currently valued at $195,000. Contributions from various family members were $145,000 over the years. Sarah has the following expenses for her first year at the university:

Tuition	$20,000
Room and board	$ 4,000
University fees	$ 900
Books for classes	$ 600
Laptop required by the university	$ 2,500
Auto to use on campus	$11,000
Total 1st year expense	$39,000

If Sarah pays for all of her expenses using a distribution from her qualified tuition plan, what effect does it have on her gross income?

14. On April 2, 2017, Clara received a refund of $4,800 from the hospital where Tim died. She had paid the hospital $5,600 late in the prior year for the medical bill and planned to add the expense to the rest of the unreimbursed medical expenses from Tim's death. Her son, Vince, told her to allow the estate to reimburse her when she paid the bill, but Clara chose to forego reimbursement. Faced with the check from the hospital, Clara fears she may have made a mistake in how she handled the expense. She consults her financial planner about the $4,800 refund. The 2016 income tax return has not been filed. How should the financial planner advise Clara?

15. George and Kathy vacationed in Guatemala in 2015 and after a visit to a local orphanage, decided to adopt a three-year-old little boy. George and Kathy felt their annual AGI of $260,000 could adequately provide for another child and that their time and cost would be greatly rewarded. Sarah is excited about her new little brother and looks forward to his arrival in the US. In February 2016, Marcus came to live with the family and his adoption became final in August 2017. The couple incurred qualified adoption costs in 2016 of $9,000 and an additional $7,500 in 2017. How much of an adoption credit can the couple use on their income tax return in 2017? Assume they file MFJ.

16. Clara is considering selling the vacation home she inherited from her mother. Her mother paid $75,000 for the home 20 years before she died and Clara inherited it. If Clara sells it today for its full fair market value of $200,000, how much would her taxable gain be on the sale of the house?

17. Assume a forest fire destroyed Clara's mountain vacation retreat in May 2017. Clara's basis in the property is $125,000. The insurance company paid Clara $226,000 in July 2017 to rebuild. Clara decided not to rebuild in such a remote area and bought a vacation home near a lake in November 2019 for $220,000. How should Clara treat the gain, if any, on this involuntary conversion?

ADDITIONAL QUESTIONS

1. List Clara's financial strengths and weaknesses.

2. After reading the case, what additional information would you request from Clara to complete your data-gathering phase?

3. Calculate the following financial ratios for Clara.

$$\frac{\text{Net Worth}}{\text{Total Assets}}$$

$$\frac{\text{Total Debt}}{\text{Total Assets}}$$

$$\frac{\text{Investment Assets}}{\text{Total Assets}}$$

4. Comment on any of the above ratios that you think are important.

5. What are Clara's options with regard to Tim's IRA?

6. Clara plans to delay the initial distribution from her IRA account until April 1, 2018. How much will she have to distribute, at a minimum, in 2018, assuming she uses the MDIB table and the IRA has the following account balances?

	2016 (Year-End)	2017 (Year-End)	2018 (Year-End)
IRA account balance	$40,000	$50,000	$60,000

7. Calculate the value of Clara's probate estate as of today, assuming the profit-sharing plan is bequeathed by Clara to George and Vince.

8. What effect does the use of community assets to pay for repairs on the vacation home property have on the titling of the vacation home at Tim's death?

9. Clara is considering establishing a charitable trust for the American Cancer Society but wants the grandchildren to receive income from the property for a 20-year period. Which devices would be appropriate to meet Clara's objective?

10. If Clara instead exercised her right to take a lump-sum cash distribution from Tim's qualified retirement plan on 1/1/17, what would be the net proceeds from the plan distribution?

11. For which Social Security benefits does Clara currently qualify?

12. What happens to Clara's IRA upon her death, assuming she makes no changes to the account?

13. How could Clara benefit each grandchild equally without incurring any transfer taxes or using her applicable exclusion amount?

14. At her death, Clara wants to maximize her benefit to the American Cancer Society and, at the same time, maximize benefits to her children and grandchildren. Which assets would be best left to the American Cancer Society?

15. Assuming that Clara has taken instead a lump-sum distribution from Tim's pension plan, what combination of investments is appropriate for Clara?

16. How much will Clara's monthly Social Security benefit be in 2017?

17. Clara is enrolled in Medicare Part B. Which benefits are covered under Medicare Part B?

18. Clara is enrolled in Medicare Part B but is still concerned about the deductibles and co-payment requirements. She is considering either purchasing a Medigap policy or joining a Medicare Advantage health maintenance organization (HMO). What are the advantages of an HMO over a Medigap policy in Clara's situation?

19. Clara is worried that she will need long-term custodial care because although her mother lived at home until age 95, she needed assistance in bathing, dressing, and toileting once she became 75 years old. Clara is worried that no family member will be around to care for her. What insurance would provide Clara with such continued assistance in her home?

20. Assume that, without telling you first, Clara takes a lump-sum distribution from Tim's qualified retirement plan. She receives a check in the amount of $120,000, which she brings to your office late on a Friday afternoon. She says she wants to roll the distribution into her IRA and asks you to make the necessary arrangements. She leaves the endorsed check with you for safekeeping. Because it is late on Friday, you deposit the check into your personal account. You plan to process the rollover next week during normal business hours. What ethical concern is raised by this scenario?

21. Assume Clara decides to take a lump-sum distribution from Tim's qualified retirement plan. You advise her to invest the proceeds in an emerging markets mutual fund that is a proprietary product of your firm. Because of a promotion your firm is running, the commission you will receive if Clara purchases the fund will exceed the commission paid on other non-proprietary funds sold by your firm. What ethical concerns are raised by your recommendation, and what must you do to address them?

22. After reviewing the documentation Clara has given you, you note in your analysis that she has only $45,000 in cash/cash equivalents but three of her stated goals are gifts to Kirby and Sarah totaling $29,000. What should you do next?

CASE

9

Michael and Michelle Williams

Michael and Michelle Williams believe they have a solid financial future; however, they are concerned about actions they need to take to ensure college educations for two of their children and a secure future for a third child with special needs. They have come to you for assistance in determining how they can achieve these goals. Today is January 1, 2017.

Personal Background and Information

Michael Williams (Age 35)

Michael is a doctor who specializes in internal medicine. He is an employee of Lakeside Hospital. The salary that Michael earns compensates him for patients seen at both the hospital and the Lakeside-owned clinic. Michael is starting his sixth year of practice. He has been discouraged lately with the medical economic environment. Given the proliferation of managed care, he sees only a limited ability to increase his salary in the future and is concerned that his salary increases are not likely to exceed inflation.

Michelle Williams (Age 35)

Michelle grew up in a middle class family and lost both of her parents to cancer in their early 50s. Michelle is a nurse but has not worked in her profession since her children were born. Michelle is fascinated with all things technological. She is a seller on an online auction site. Michelle has an uncanny sense for shopping for unique items that she buys, adds a markup, and resells. She marks up an item 100%, does not sell the item for less than its marked-up price, and charges the online buyer for all related shipping costs. For 2017, she has changed the dynamic of her business and expects to generate up to $90,000 net income after expenses from the business this year.

Children

Michelle and Michael have three children: Beau (age 7), Elizabeth (age 5), and Madison (age 2). Madison has Down syndrome.

Michael's Family

Michael is an only child and has been his parents' pride and joy. Michael's parents (Frank and Isabelle) are first-generation immigrants from England. They immigrated before Michael was born and operate a small neighborhood deli. Michael and Michelle met at the deli when Michelle worked there during her college years. The ebb and flow of community life through the deli still fascinates Michelle, and she often visits Michael's parents there. The elder Williamses own the building (fair market value, $250,000) that houses the deli. The neighborhood has seen needed renovations in recent years, and the future outlook for continued renewal is good. The deli enjoys a steady stream of loyal customers and has generated moderate wealth for Michael's parents. They are both 60 years old and are in fair health. Frank and Isabelle have no family in this country except for Michael. As they approach retirement, their primary concerns are the high costs of long-term residential and medical care for the elderly.

Michelle's Family

Michelle's parents are both deceased. Michelle is close to her only sibling, Joan (age 40). Joan is unmarried and has no children. Joan is particularly close to the Williamses' children. In the past, Joan has mentioned to Michelle that she would consider assisting with the educational and maintenance needs of the children. Joan has given up her job as a business education teacher to be a full-time author of financial self-help books and works out of her home. To date she has enjoyed tremendous success and has raised her annual income from $35,000 a year to $100,000.

Personal and Financial Objectives

1. The Williamses want to provide Beau and Elizabeth with up to $25,000 (today's dollars) per year for four years of college education. The children will be on their own for the costs of any graduate studies.

2. They want to assist Michael's parents in their retirement years, as needed.

3. They want to be free of mortgage indebtedness by the time Michael is 55 years old.

4. They want to design a retirement plan that will provide an income to replace 70% of Michael's preretirement income.

5. They want to make necessary arrangements for Madison so that she will be cared for throughout her adult life.

6. They want to maintain an adequate emergency fund of six months' living expenses.

7. They want to prepare proper wills and an estate plan.

Economic Information

■ They expect inflation to average 3%.

■ They expect an educational consumer price index (CPI) of 5%.

■ They expect Michael's salary to increase 3% annually.

- ■ Rates are 7% for a 15-year fixed mortgage and 7.5% for a 30-year fixed mortgage.

- ■ They are in a 28% federal income tax bracket and a 6% state income tax bracket.

Any refinancing will incur 3% of the mortgage as a closing cost which will not be financed.

Insurance Information

Health Insurance

Health insurance is provided for the entire immediate family through Lakeside Hospital. Lakeside Hospital's health insurance is through a preferred provider organization (PPO). The contract has a family deductible of $500 per year. If preferred contract physicians are used, the contract is an 80/20 major medical coinsurance plan. The family annual stop-loss limit is $2,000. Prescription drug, eye, or dental coverage is not included in the plan. The plan has unlimited lifetime benefits.

Life Insurance

Michael has elected $50,000 group term life insurance through the hospital. The hospital pays the entire premium. Michelle has maintained a $10,000 whole life insurance policy her parents purchased for her as a child. The cash value of the policy is $6,000 and the policy is paid up.

Disability Insurance

The hospital does not provide disability insurance for its employed physicians. Michael has purchased a policy through the American Medical Association. The policy provides own-occupation coverage for disability resulting from either sickness or accident, pays a benefit of 60% of gross pay after an elimination period of 180 days, covers a term of 60 months with residual benefits, and is guaranteed renewable.

Malpractice Insurance

The hospital provides Michael with malpractice insurance and pays the premium. The policy covers Michael's work at both the hospital and in the clinical practice.

Homeowners Insurance

The Williamses currently have an HO-3 policy with a replacement value on contents endorsement. The deductible is $250 with a premium of $2,000 per year.

Automobile Insurance

Michael and Michelle have full coverage on both cars, including:

- $100,000 bodily injury for one person
- $300,000 bodily injury for all persons
- $50,000 property damage
- $100,000 uninsured motorist
- $10,000 medical payments

Deductibles are:

- $500 comprehensive
- $1,000 collision

Investment Information (Assumptions)

	Expected Return	Beta
Aggressive stocks	13.5%	1.7
Growth stocks	10%	1.2
S&P 500 Index	9%	1.0
Value stocks	8.5%	0.9
Bonds (corporate)	6.5%	0.6
Money market (bank)	1.75%	0.2

The Williamses consider themselves to be moderate risk-taking investors.

Retirement Information

Michael and Michelle would like to retire on or before age 67. They both expect to live to age 92. They would like to have a standard of living equal to 70% of their preretirement income. They do not want to rely on Social Security benefits in planning for their retirement.

During the past year, Michael began participating in a Section 401(k) plan available through Lakeside Hospital. Under the plan, the hospital matches $.50 for every dollar contributed, up to 6% of his salary. The maximum contribution by the hospital is a total of 3%. The plan allows for deferrals up to a maximum of 7% of salary.

Gifts, Estates, Trusts, and Will Information

Neither Michael nor Michelle has a will. They realize the importance of having a will; however, Michael's schedule seems to preclude any time for finalizing one. They are most concerned about guardian care for Madison, while at the same time minimizing as much estate tax as possible.

STATEMENT OF CASH FLOWS
Michael and Michelle Williams
For the Year Ended December 31, 2016

CASH INFLOWS

Salary—Michael	$170,000	
Gift from Michael's parents	20,000	
Michelle's self-employment income	4,000	
Interest	900	
Total inflows		**$194,900**

CASH OUTFLOWS

Section 401(k) plan savings	$ 11,900	
Mortgage payment	20,700	
Property taxes (residence)	1,800	
FICA and self-employment tax	9,820	
Federal income tax withholding	68,000	
State income tax withholding	6,734	
Utilities	3,980	
Disability insurance premium	900	
Homeowners insurance	2,000	
Auto notes	10,789	
Auto expense and maintenance	1,200	
Auto insurance	2,400	
Housekeeping service	2,400	
Educational loan repayment	6,915	
Clothing and dry cleaning	5,600	
Food	5,750	
Entertainment	3,970	
Miscellaneous	5,998	
Total outflows		**$170,856**
Net cash flow (surplus)		**$ 24,044**

STATEMENT OF FINANCIAL POSITION
Michael and Michelle Williams
January 1, 2017

Assets[1]			Liabilities and Net Worth[2]	
Cash/cash equivalents			**Current liabilities**	
Checking account	JT	$2,500	Credit card balances	$ 550
Money market account[3]	JT	5,000	Auto loan (Audi)	25,000
(1.75% interest rate)			Auto loan (Toyota)	18,000
Total cash/cash equivalents		**$7,500**	*Total current liabilities*	**$43,550**
Invested assets			**Long-term liabilities**	
CD	JT	$15,000	Home mortgage	$225,000
Section 401(k) plan	S1	10,000	Student loans	50,500
Cash value of life insurance	S2	6,000		
Coin collection	S1	10,000	**Total long-term liabilities**	**$275,500**
Total investments		**$41,000**		
Personal use assets			Net worth	**$73,950**
House (appraised 7/01/13)[4]	JT	$275,000		
Auto (Toyota)	JT	22,500		
Auto (Audi)	JT	47,000		
Total personal use		**$344,500**		
Total assets		**$393,000**	**Total liabilities and net worth**	**$393,000**

Note to financial statements
[1]Assets are stated at fair market value.
[2]Liabilities are stated at principal only and are all joint obligations except the student loans which belong to Michael.
[3]The money market account is currently serving as their emergency fund.
[4]Land value was determined to be $50,000 and the home value $225,000. Replacement value of the home is also $225,000.
Title designations
JT = Joint tenancy with right of survivorship
S1 = Michael's separate property
S2 = Michelle's separate property

The Williamses primarily use cash, check, and debit cards for personal expenditures.

QUESTIONS

1. Assume that Michelle is self-employed. What are her retirement plan options?

2. By using the annuity approach, calculate the capital needed at retirement (age 67) for the Williamses. Assume a 9% after-tax rate of return. Base the calculation on Michael's salary only.

3. By using the capital preservation approach, calculate the capital needed at retirement for the Williamses.

4. By using the purchasing power preservation approach, calculate the capital needed at retirement for the Williamses.

5. Explain the key differences among the three approaches in Questions 2–4.

6. Use the capital need you calculated in Question 2 to determine whether the Williamses will be able to retire at age 67 with their current annual savings. For current annual savings, use Michael's Section 401(k) plan contribution plus the employer's match and assume that Michelle saves all that she currently earns on an annual basis. Do not use Michelle's projected earnings; rather, use her current earnings. Assume that all investment assets (regardless of how they are currently invested) will earn a 9% after-tax rate of return. Consider the checking account, money market account, and coin collection as nonretirement assets.

7. What changes, if any, would you recommend to the Williamses regarding their retirement planning? For example, if they are not currently projected to meet their goal, how much additional annual savings will be required? Is there any other potential source of retirement income they could consider?

8. If Michael and Michelle include the receipt of Social Security benefits in their retirement planning, could they retire at age 67 without increasing their annual savings? Assume that at age 67 (in today's dollars) Michael's Social Security benefit would be $29,820 and Michelle's would be $14,910. Use Michael's salary only.

9. If the Williamses choose to rely on Social Security benefits in their retirement planning, how much earlier than age 67 can they retire? (Assume all other facts as given in Question 8).

Use the following information for questions 10 through 14.

Michelle's online auction business has taken off this year, and she had to hire two employees. She has a website on which she sells products in a manner similar to other stores. The most unusual and valuable items in her inventory are available through internet auction only. Her store is linked to the online auction website and several search engines. She is projecting net income of $90,000 from the business in 2017. Michelle wants to keep her workforce stable by offering them benefits, including a retirement plan. More importantly, she needs to maximize her retirement savings in order to help meet their retirement goals. She does not want to factor the increase in her business income into their retirement needs calculations. Both Michelle and Michael believe the plan based primarily on his income will be sufficient for their retirement. Michelle wants to make contributions to the employees' retirement accounts as a benefit to them. She has heard about the testing of retirement plans and wants a plan that will minimize the testing and administration burden. Her two employees make $20,000 and $25,000 each. She is considering a qualified defined contribution plan for the self-employed, a SEP IRA, a SIMPLE IRA, and a SIMPLE 401(k).

10. Describe a qualified defined contribution plan for the self-employed and discuss the advantages and disadvantages in adopting this type of plan.

11. Describe a SEP IRA and discuss the advantages and disadvantages in adopting this type of plan.

12. Describe a SIMPLE IRA and discuss the advantages and disadvantages in adopting this type of plan.

13. Describe a SIMPLE 401(k) and discuss the advantages and disadvantages in adopting this type of plan.

14. Of the four plans discussed, which is the best fit for Michelle's new business?

ADDITIONAL QUESTIONS

1. List the Williamses' financial strengths and weaknesses.

2. What additional information would you request from the Williamses to complete your data-gathering phase?

3. Comment on the Williamses' use of debt.

4. Assuming a 9% after-tax rate of return, calculate the amount needed today to fund the children's college education.

5. By using life insurance industry rules of thumb, how much life insurance should Michael carry?

6. In general, what issues must be decided when purchasing a long-term care insurance policy?

7. Frank and Isabelle are thinking of retiring in five years and are considering transferring the deli to Michelle. They believe that such a transfer would be wise, for it would remove the value of the deli from their gross estate. They are wondering what the value of the deli might be today using the capitalized earnings model.

   Calculate the value of the deli assuming the deli generates earnings before taxes of $150,000 annually and a capitalization rate of 18%. Add in the cost of the business real estate.

8. Frank and Isabelle have identified five possible ways that they could effect the transfer of the deli to Michelle. Describe the transfer method and the advantages and disadvantages to the parties.
   a. Outright gift
   b. Private annuity
   c. Self-canceling installment note (SCIN)
   d. Grantor retained annuity trust
   e. Family limited partnership

9. The Williamses wish to establish a special needs trust for Madison. What factors and benefits should be included in such a trust? How should it be funded?

10. Assume that the state in which they live has a fairly onerous probate system. What can the Williamses do to avoid probate?

11. Michael and Michelle wish to refinance their home mortgage. Will they qualify for the 15-year or the 30-year mortgage? What will be the total principal and interest payments for the 15-year and the 30-year mortgage?

12. Are there federal income tax implications regarding the group term life insurance benefit that Michael receives from the hospital if the coverage is increased to two times his salary? Be sure to include any calculated amounts, and say how and where they would be reported.

13. Lakeside Hospital has just begun offering employees a flexible spending account (FSA) benefit. Michael is considering contributing to the FSA for assistance in covering child-care costs. Recently, however, a CPA friend of Michael's told him about the federal income tax dependent care credit. Assume that Michael approaches you, a financial planner, for advice on which approach would be best to use—FSA or the dependent care credit. Can the Williamses use both the FSA and the dependent care credit?

14. If Michelle only conducts a few online auction transactions, will the transactions qualify as a trade or business? Discuss the income tax consequences of Michelle's online auction transactions assuming: a) the transactions do not constitute a trade or business, and b) the transactions do constitute a trade or business. For each alternative, specify how transaction gains and losses would be treated for federal income tax purposes, and identify the tax schedule on which the activity would be reported.

15. Assuming a 9% after-tax rate of return, calculate the amount the Williamses need to save annually at year-end to fund the children's college education. Assume payments are made until the second child starts college.

16. What are the Williamses' present insurance portfolio deficiencies?

17. Using a human value approach net of state and federal income taxes and assuming a 9% after-tax rate of return, how much additional life insurance is needed on Michael's life?

18. Michelle's sister wishes to pay for Madison's schooling and medical costs. How can she pay these costs so the payment is not considered a taxable gift?

19. Assume that Michael's Section 401(k) plan balance is equally invested in two mutual funds. Mutual Fund A has a standard deviation of 8%, and Mutual Fund B has a standard deviation of 11%. Assume the correlation coefficient of the funds is 75%. Calculate the standard deviation of the two-asset portfolio.

20. What is the residual benefits feature in Michael's disability policy?

21. Should Frank and Isabelle Williams purchase a long-term care insurance policy? Would any premiums paid for the long-term care policy be income tax deductible?

22. In the order of importance, what are the ten primary actions the Williamses should take immediately regarding their financial security?

23. What issues are involved in the selection of a guardian for Michael and Michelle's children?

24. Using the financial needs approach and assuming the following expenses, what is the minimum amount of life insurance Michelle should have today to protect the family?

    - Final expenses of $20,000

    - Annual childcare costs of $15,000 per year for 10 years

    - College funding for Beau ($62,721) and Elizabeth ($58,202)

    - Mortgage of $225,000

    - Auto loans of $43,000

    - Student loans of $50,500

    - Credit card debt of $550

    - Return on invested money is 9%

    - Expected inflation rate is 3%

    - Emergency fund need of roughly $23,064 ($30,564 need – $7,500 cash)

25. If the Williamses average $2,000 in annual dental and vision care expenses, how much would they save/exclude from taxes by using pretax dollars?

26. Other than child care costs and unreimbursed medical expenses, what expenses can Michael pay for with pretax dollars through his FSA?

27. Frank and Isabelle have told Michelle of the various ways they could transfer the deli to her. They are currently favoring making an outright gift to Michelle but Michelle is not certain that is the best alternative to use. Michelle and Michael are concerned about the possibility that they will need to provide some support to Michael's parents in the future and believe that the income from the deli could provide his parents with the support they need. Michelle has brought the various alternatives that Michael's parents were given by their planner and would like you to review them and help the Williames decide which alternative would best transfer the business while also satisfying the Williamses' goal of providing needed support to Frank and Isabelle. What should you do next?

28. Assume you recommend that Michelle implement a SEP IRA and she accepts your recommendation. Your firm has relationships with several SEP administrators but is a "preferred supplier" for one of them. "Preferred supplier" status means your firm receives greater compensation for directing clients to this administrator than to others. What ethical issues are raised if you direct Michelle to this SEP administrator, and what must you do to address them?

29. Assume that during your planning relationship with the Williamses, Michael and Michelle begin to disagree strongly about some of their objectives. Michael wants to devote more of their resources to helping his parents, while Michelle is more concerned with their own retirement and providing for Madison's future needs. Michelle feels she should have more input into their planning because her business is starting to take off and her income may soon exceed Michael's. Michael has previously indicated his satisfaction with your services and has said he plans to refer some of his physician friends to you, so you do not want to disrupt your good relationship with him. You are also good friends with his parents, and they have frequently asked you about the Williamses' plans. What ethical concerns are raised by this scenario?

10

Robert and Lisa Franklin

Today's date is January 1, 2017. Robert and Lisa Franklin have come to you, a financial planner, for help in developing a plan to accomplish their financial goals. From your initial meeting together, you have gathered the following information.

Personal Background and Information

Robert Franklin (Age 65)

Robert Franklin's date of birth is January 2, 1951. He was employed for 20 years as a partner at Franklin Securities (Franklin). He participates in a Keogh plan at Franklin. He was previously employed for 20 years as a broker with Smith Brothers, Inc., where he participated in a Section 401(k) plan.

Lisa Franklin (Age 65)

Lisa Franklin's date of birth is January 10, 1951. She has volunteered at Children's Hospital and the American Red Cross for the past 15 years.

The Franklins

They have been married 42 years. Both Robert and Lisa are currently in good health, although Robert had a mild heart attack eight years ago. Their joint life expectancy is 26.2 years.

Children

Child	Age	Grandchildren
Pam	39	Two children
Elise	36	Five children
Jackie	30	Four children
Vicki	29	Three children
Robert Jr.	18	No children

All of the daughters are healthy, employed, married, and not living with Robert and Lisa. Robert Jr. is unemployed, single, a high school graduate, and lives with his parents until he begins college in the fall.

Personal and Financial Objectives

1. Robert plans to retire now and travel around the world with Lisa.

2. Robert plans to sell his share of the securities business. He wants to sell half of his share to his key employee, Mark Newhart. He wants to sell the other half to his daughter, Elise, who is the senior broker in the firm.

3. After traveling around the world, Robert plans to return to the business as a self-employed consultant on a fee basis beginning January 1, 2018.

4. Robert Jr. will be starting at a private university in the fall of 2017.

5. Robert's grandchild, Greg, Pam's youngest child, was born with a serious physical disability. Robert plans to give Greg $2.5 million through a trust for his care and benefit.

Economic Information

- The couple expects inflation to average 4% annually. The expected stock market returns are 10% annually, as measured by the S&P 500 Index, with a standard deviation of 15%.

- Tuition is currently $30,000 per year at the private university. The expected education inflation rate is 5%.

- The 90-day T-bill is yielding 3.5%. The 30-year Treasury bond is yielding 7.5%.

- Current mortgage rates are 7.5% for 15 years and 8.0% for 30 years. In addition, closing costs (3% of the mortgage) will be paid at closing and not financed.

Insurance Information

Life Insurance

Neither spouse has life insurance.

Health Insurance

Robert's business provides health coverage for both Lisa and himself during employment and retirement.

- Major medical coverage
- 80/20 coinsurance clause
- $250 deductible per person
- $2,000 family stop-loss provision

Disability Insurance

Neither Robert nor Lisa has disability insurance.

Homeowners Insurance

They have HO-3 policies on their primary residence and vacation homes. The vacation homes are located on the U.S. Gulf Coast and in the mountains.

	Residence	Vacation Home U.S. Gulf Coast	Vacation Home Mountains
Dwelling	$975,000	$700,000	$600,000
Coinsurance requirement	80%	80%	80%
Deductible—all other covered losses	$250	$250	$250
Deductible—hurricane	n/a	$10,500	n/a

Personal Liability Umbrella Policy

They have $5 million of coverage.

Automobile Insurance

They have liability coverage, $250,000/$500,000/$100,000. They also carry comprehensive and collision on their autos.

Insurance Premiums

- Car insurance: $6,000 per year for all three of Robert and Lisa's automobiles

- Homeowners insurance: $8,500 per year (includes all homes)

- Boat insurance: $1,200 per year (covered under the umbrella policy)

- Umbrella policy: $1,000 per year

Investment Information

- The Franklins have a required rate of return of 8%.

- The couple can tolerate medium to high amounts of risk but have little need to take excessive risks because of their net worth.

- Robert's Section 401(k) plan investments are in a well-diversified but relatively volatile group of small-cap value stocks. The funds in his Section 401(k) plan are still in Smith Brothers' Retirement Plan.

- Robert has a single premium deferred annuity that was purchased on July 1, 1985, for $60,000 and is currently worth $233,047. The expected return over the next year and the 15 years of the fixed term of the annuity is 6%. The start date of the monthly annuity is January 1, 2018, when the expected fair market value will be $247,030.

- Robert plans to sell 4,468 shares of Dollar Mart stock to his daughter, Vicki, who is employed by Dollar Mart. Robert anticipates the stock will greatly appreciate in future years. (The stock was purchased in 2011 for $26.66 per share and is currently trading for $11.25 per share.)

Income Tax Information

- Robert and Lisa are in the highest federal income tax bracket (39.6% marginal rate).

- They also pay state income taxes of 5%.

- For personal income tax reporting, Robert has a $700,000 salary.

- They do not reside in a community property state.

Retirement Information

- The Section 401(k) plan has a balance of $600,000 consisting of a portfolio of small-cap value stocks. The portfolio is projected to average a return of 16% over the next 20 years with a standard deviation of 8%.

- Robert's anticipated Social Security retirement benefit is $24,000 per year in 2017 and will increase at the expected consumer price index (CPI) of 4%.

- Robert has a profit-sharing type of self-employed qualified plan. His company contributes $12,000 per year to the plan. The contributions to this plan have been made out of the company's profits. The balance in his account is a result of an annual contribution of $12,000, with a 7% approximate average rate of return.

- Robert and Lisa will continue to collect $200,000 per year in rental proceeds from Commercial Property A.

- Robert will receive $50,000 per year from the charitable remainder annuity trust (CRAT) that owns Commercial Property B for Robert's lifetime.

Gifts, Estates, Trusts, and Will Information

Gifts

The following are the Franklins' only lifetime gifts.

■ For the past several years, Robert has given cash gifts to each of his five children. Each gift has been equal to the annual exclusion amount for the year of the gift, so no taxable gifts have resulted.

■ Robert is planning to transfer $3 million of property to a grantor retained annuity trust (GRAT) in 2017. Robert hopes to save on gift and estate taxes by transferring this portion of his interest into a trust while retaining the right to a fixed ordinary annuity of $298,059 for a term of 10 years. The Franklins' five children will be the remainder beneficiaries of the GRAT. Upon the death of a remainderman, the interest will pass to the remainderman's descendants. If a remainderman dies without heirs, then the remainderman's interest will pass to the other children (remaindermen) pro rata. Based on recent Section 7520 rates, Robert expects the taxable gift resulting from the transfer will be $1 million.

■ Lisa has made no taxable gifts during her lifetime nor have any gifts been split.

■ In 2016, Robert established a 5% CRAT by donating a piece of real estate (an apartment building, Commercial Property B) inherited from his grandfather. The initial valuation of the trust was $1 million with the initial income in the first year projected to be $50,000 beginning in 2017. Robert is the income beneficiary, and the charitable remainder beneficiary is the Chicago Art Institute.

■ Robert plans to donate $2.5 million to an irrevocable trust for his grandchild, Greg, the youngest child of Pam. During one of your meetings with the Franklins, you offer to serve as trustee of this trust. When they ask you what your fee will be, you reply that you are not sure yet but it will be slightly lower than the standard trustee fee in your area. They do not ask about the fee again.

Estates

The Franklins' last illness and funeral expenses combined with estate administration expenses are estimated at $450,000 each.

Wills

Robert and Lisa have simple wills. They have left all probate assets to each other. Each will also include a six-month survivorship clause. Debts and taxes are to be paid from the residue of the estate.

Will

Excerpts from Robert Franklin's Last Will and Testament

I, ROBERT FRANKLIN SR., being of sound mind and wishing to make proper disposition of my property in the event of my death, do declare this to be my Last Will and Testament. I revoke all of my prior wills and codicils.

1.1	I have been married but once, and only to Lisa Franklin with whom I am presently living.
1.2	Out of my marriage to Lisa Franklin, five children were born namely Pam Franklin, Elise Franklin, Jackie Franklin, Vicki Franklin, and Robert Franklin Jr.
1.3	I have adopted no one nor has anyone adopted me.

3.1	I give my entire estate to Lisa Franklin, my wife.
3.2	In the event that Lisa Franklin predeceases me or fails to survive me for more than six months from the date of my death, I give my entire estate to my children Pam Franklin, Elise Franklin, Jackie Franklin, Vicki Franklin, and Robert Franklin Jr., in equal and undivided one-fifth shares.
3.3	In the event that any of the named heirs or legatees should predecease me, die within six months from the date of my death, disclaim or otherwise fail to accept any property bequeath to him and said legatee has no descendants, his share of all of my property of which I die possessed shall be given to the surviving named legatees.

5.1	I name Lisa Franklin to serve as my executrix of my succession, with full seisin and without bond.
5.2	I direct that the expenses of my last illness, funeral, and the administration of my estate shall be paid by my executrix as soon as practicable after my death.
5.3	All inheritance, estate, succession, transfer, and other taxes (including interest and penalties thereon) payable by reason of my death shall be apportioned in accordance with the law.

STATEMENT OF CASH FLOWS
Robert and Lisa Franklin
January 1, 2016, to December 31, 2016

CASH INFLOWS		
Salary		
Robert's salary	$700,000	
Total salary		$700,000
Rental income		200,000
Dividend income		
Robert	5,000	
Lisa	1,500	
Total dividend income		6,500
Interest income[1]		1,000
Total income		$907,500
CASH OUTFLOWS		
Mortgage payments		
Primary residence	$ 37,030	
Vacation home 1	45,181	
Vacation home 2	79,308	
Total mortgage payments		$161,519
Insurance Premiums		
Homeowners	$ 8,500	
Auto	6,000	
Boat	1,200	
Umbrella	1,000	
Total insurance premiums		$ 16,700
Misc. expenses		
Credit card payments	$ 2,400	
Entertainment	50,000	
Food	14,400	
Clothes	30,000	
Utilities	24,000	
Charity	90,000	
Total misc. expenses		$210,800
Tax		
Property tax	$ 84,000	
Income tax	408,375	
Total tax		$492,375
Total outflows		$881,394
Net cash flow (surplus)		$ 26,106

Notes to financial statements
[1] Because the initial income from the CRAT of $50,000 is projected for January 1, 2017 (for CRAT income earned in 2016), it was omitted from the 2016 Statement of Cash Flows.

STATEMENT OF FINANCIAL POSITION
Robert and Lisa Franklin
As of January 1, 2017

Assets[1]			Liabilities and Net Worth		
			Liabilities[2]		
Cash/cash equivalents			**Current liabilities**		
JT	Cash	$ 100,000	S2	Credit card 1	$ 1,000
			S2	Credit card 2	15,000
	Total cash/cash equivalents	$ 100,000		Total current liabilities	$ 16,000
Invested assets			**Long-term liabilities**		
JT	Franklin Securities	$ 5,000,000	JT	Mortgage—primary	$ 258,630
S2	Lisa's portfolio	500,000	JT	Mortgage—vac GC	369,428
S1	Deferred annuity	233,047	JT	Mortgage—vac mts	687,444
S1	Section 401(k) plan (vested balance)	600,000			
S1	Profit-sharing plan (vested balance)	526,382		Total long-term liabilities	$ 1,315,502
S1	Robert's portfolio	4,000,000			
JT	Commercial Property A	1,500,000		Total liabilities	$ 1,331,502
	Total investments	$12,359,429			
Personal use assets				Net worth	$15,087,927
JT	Primary residence	$ 1,300,000			
JT	Vacation home—U.S. Gulf Coast	800,000			
JT	Vacation home—mountains	700,000			
JT	Personal property/furniture	875,000			
S1	Auto 1	80,000			
S1	Auto 2	55,000			
S2	Auto 3	40,000			
S2	Boat	110,000			
	Total personal use assets	$ 3,960,000			
	Total assets	$16,419,429		Total liabilities and net worth	$16,419,429

Notes to financial statements
[1]Assets are stated at fair market value (rounded to whole dollars).
[2]Liabilities are stated at principal only (rounded to whole dollars).

Title designations
JT - Joint tenancy with right of survivorship
S1 - Robert's separate
S2 - Lisa's separate

Information Regarding Assets and Liabilities

Franklin Securities (Robert is a 50% partner)

- The fair market value of Robert's interest is $5 million.

- Robert's current adjusted tax basis is $1 million.

- Details of the transfer of the business (sale) are as follows.

  — 50%: a 10-year installment sale to Mark Newhart for a down payment of 20% on January 1, 2017, and monthly payments beginning February 1, 2017, at 10% annual interest

  — 50%: self-canceling installment note (SCIN) or private annuity to Elise

Primary Residence

- Purchased in 2001

- Jointly owned (joint tenants with right of survivorship)

- Market value $1.3 million

- Original purchase price $300,000

- Current mortgage at 12% interest; monthly payment: $3,085.84 (30 year)

Vacation Home—U.S. Gulf Coast

- Jointly owned; purchased in 2014

- Market value $800,000

- Original purchase price $400,000

- Current mortgage at 7.75%; monthly payment: $3,765.10 (15 year)

Vacation Home—Mountains

- Jointly owned; purchased in 2016

- Market value $700,000

- Original purchase price $700,000

- Current mortgage at 7.8%; monthly payment: $6,608.99 (15 year)

Commercial Property A

- Original site of the business
- Fair market value $1.5 million
- Adjusted basis $200,000

Single Premium Deferred Annuity

- Robert purchased this annuity on July 1, 1985, for $60,000. The current fair market value is $233,047.

- An earnings rate of 6% compounded annually is expected in the near term.

- Annuity start date is January 1, 2018, at which time the fair market value is projected to be $247,030 and will consist of 180 monthly payments (15 years).

- If Robert dies before the annuity start date, Lisa is named beneficiary (100% joint and survivor annuity).

Summary of Indebtedness

Asset	Date 1st Payment	Amount of Mortgage	Term/ Years	Interest	Monthly Payments	Remaining Payments	Remaining Balance
Primary residence	4/1/01	$300,000	30	12.00%	($3,085.84)	183	$ 258,629.70
Vacation home GC	1/1/14	$400,000	15	7.75%	($3,765.10)	156	$ 369,427.86
Vacation home mts	7/1/16	$700,000	15	7.80%	($6,608.99)	174	$ 687,443.56
							$1,315,501.12

Detailed Investment Portfolios

Robert's Portfolio

Description	Acquired	Shares	Adjusted Basis	Beta	Current FMV
Sears	8/08	16,325	$201,633	0.9	$ 830,214
Dollar Mart	1/11	4,468	$119,117	1.2	$ 50,265
Canon, Inc.	2/13	22,249	$400,188	1.4	$2,230,462
*RC, Inc.	9/13	3,742	$ 67,181	1.5	$ 222,600
WW Grainger	10/16	4,257	$221,435	1.2	$ 311,293
City Electronics stores	9/16	10,561	$304,062	1.2	$ 355,166
					$4,000,000

*The RC, Inc., stock is Section 1244 Small Business Stock. The beta is determined by industry standards.

Lisa's Portfolio

Description	Acquired	Shares	Adjusted Basis	Beta	Current FMV
Tenet Health Care	1/08	2,542	$ 30,504	0.6	$ 50,209
Bay Bank, Inc.	2/13	1,500	$120,000	0.5	$167,250
Microsoft	9/13	589	$ 53,010	0.7	$ 66,189
Zenith	10/14	22,190	$177,520	0.8	$216,352
					$500,000

QUESTIONS

1. Assume Lisa dies on January 1, 2017.
   a. What is the value of Lisa's gross estate?
   b. What amount qualifies for the marital deduction in Lisa's estate assuming Robert survives for 6 months following her death?
   c. Determine whether Lisa's estate is overqualified or underqualified and suggest any estate tax elections Lisa's personal representative might make to help alleviate the effects of the overqualification or underqualification.

2. Which of the following transfers will not result in a taxable gift from Robert in 2017, assuming he makes no other gifts?
   a. Robert pays each grandchild's private school tuition ($6,000 each).
   b. Robert pays City Hospital for the hospital bill of a friend ($15,000).
   c. Robert pays a university for a distant cousin's law school tuition ($16,000).
   d. Robert pays the tuition for Robert Jr. directly to a private university ($30,000).

3. What is the impact of the survivorship clause in Robert's will?

4. Robert and Lisa are considering the purchase of a joint and survivor (second-to-die) life insurance policy for the purpose of wealth replacement for the assets that were transferred to the CRAT and to help to create estate liquidity. Discuss the most appropriate way to own the joint and survivor life insurance.

5. What estate planning recommendations would you make to the Franklins?

6. Explain the benefits of the grantor retained annuity trust (GRAT) Robert is planning to create in 2017.

7. What are the advantages of using a charitable remainder trust (CRT)?

8. Discuss private annuities and SCINS and how the use of each would affect Robert Franklin and his daughter Elise in the sale of half of his share of Franklin Securities to her instead of in an installment sale.

9. If the Franklins set up an irrevocable trust for the rest of their grandchildren, what kind of tax will the grandchildren pay on the income distributed to them from this trust?

ADDITIONAL QUESTIONS

1. List the Franklins' financial strengths and weaknesses.

2. After reading the case, what additional information would you request from the Franklins to complete your data-gathering phase?

3. Assume that Robert sells the Dollar Mart stock to Vicki for the current fair market value. What are Robert's tax consequences from this transaction?

4. Assume that Robert sells the Dollar Mart stock to Vicki for the fair market value as of January 1, 2017, and Vicki resells the Dollar Mart stock at $16.50 per share on December 15, 2017. What are the income tax consequences to Vicki?

5. What is the tax treatment if Robert sells all of his RC, Inc. stock this year at the current fair market value?

6. Assume that on August 15, 2017, Robert has the following sales in his stock portfolio. Assume that these are the Franklins' only stock transactions for the year.

Sale Date	Stock	Number of Shares	Sale Price Net Commissions
8/15/17	Sears	16,325	$840,000
8/15/17	WW Grainger	4,257	$320,000
8/15/17	Circuit City	10,561	$190,000

What are the income tax consequences of these transactions?

7. Evaluate the adequacy of Robert and Lisa's insurance plans. Assume that the replacement value of their primary residence is $1.5 million.

8. Assuming that Robert begins his single premium deferred annuity on the start date of January 1, 2018, what will be his tax consequences from the annuity payments received in 2018?

9. In 2018, when Robert returns from traveling and begins his consulting career, he expects to have taxable earned income of $100,000 per year. Describe the impact of his consulting activities on Social Security benefits and the taxation of Social Security benefits received.

10. Using the capital asset pricing model, determine the expected dollar return for Lisa's portfolio, assuming the market has a return 20% better than expected.

11. If the Franklins were to refinance their primary residence at current mortgage rates for 15 years, how much would their monthly payment decline?

12. In 2018, Robert will begin his consulting. Discuss his ability to defer taxes by using a qualified retirement plan.

13. Regarding the installment sale portion of the interest in Franklin Securities to Mark Newhart, how much, if any, of the down payment is taxable to the Franklins in 2017, and what is the character of the down payment?

14. Rounding to the nearest dollar, calculate the total monthly installment payments that will be made to the Franklins by Newhart during 2017.

15. In 2017, how much will Robert have to claim as ordinary income from the installment sale of Franklin Securities?

16. Robert has paid his general liability insurance premiums for Franklin Securities for 2 years in advance. The premium for the 2 years was $144,000. At the time of his sale of the firm to Elise and Newhart, there will be a prepaid insurance amount. Robert plans to assign the insurance policy to the new partnership of Elise and Newhart and wants them to pay him for the remaining prepaid insurance premiums. Discuss the validity and effectiveness of the assignment of the policy.

17. What is the likelihood Robert's Section 401(k) plan will provide a return that is below the Franklins' required rate of return?

18. What investment planning recommendations would you make to the Franklins?

19. Approximately how much will the Franklins have to set aside today to fund tuition for Robert Jr. for 6 years at the university if he begins attending in 2017?

20. Because the Franklins will be traveling for the next year, they will not be using the vacation homes. The vacation home on the Gulf Coast in particular is used by the Franklins as their children all prefer the larger vacation home in the mountains. The couple is considering renting the house to vacationers for at least the next year. How would the rental income affect the Franklins' income tax return for 2017?

21. The Franklins have decided to sell the vacation home on the Gulf Coast, instead of renting it to others, for the FMV of $800,000. They have owned the home and used it for vacations since 2014. How much of the gain on the sale of the home can the couple exclude from gross income in 2017, the year the sale is finalized?

22. What steps should the Franklins take now concerning Social Security and Medicare?

23. While driving home from work, Robert gets into a car accident with a deer that causes $1,500 in damage to his vehicle. In addition, after hitting the deer, Robert's car careens off the road and into a neighbor's garage, causing $12,500 worth of damage to the structure. What is the amount of insurance that Robert's policy will pay regarding the two incidents?

24. After receiving the documentation on the installment sale and the SCIN for the sale of Robert's business interest, you realize that with the CRAT, the proposed GRAT, Commercial Property A, and the business sale, the Franklins will, for a period of several years, have a greater annual income than they presently enjoy. What should you do next?

25. Assume Robert implements the $2.5 million irrevocable trust for Greg and appoints you as trustee. What additional disclosures, if any, must you make to the Franklins regarding your service as trustee?

26. Assume that during your planning relationship with the Franklins, you establish a client-planner relationship with Mark Newhart. Mark tells you he is interested in obtaining a majority interest in Franklin Securities rather than the 50% interest envisioned by Robert's current plan for the disposition of the business. He knows Elise also wants to control the business. Mark asks you to convince Robert to revise his plan for the business so Mark will receive a 51% interest and Elise will receive a 49% interest. He says that if you do, he will refer clients of the securities business to you for financial planning. During a subsequent meeting with Robert, you do not disclose your relationship with Mark but you tell Robert that 50-50 ownership interests often result in management deadlock when the owners disagree and that because Mark is a key employee and has more experience than Elise, it might be wise to give him operating control of the business. What ethical issues are raised by this scenario, and what must you do to address them?

Appendix

List of Exhibits

Exhibit 1: The Financial Planning Process

1. Establishing and Defining the Client-Planner Relationship.

2. Gathering Information Necessary to Fulfill the Engagement.
   a. Personal information about client and family.
   b. Current personal financial statements, which include statement of cash flows and statement of financial position.
   c. Personal and business tax returns (5 years).
   d. Insurance policies (health, life, disability, auto, homeowners, and umbrella).
   e. Employee benefits booklets and reports.
   f. Descriptions in detail regarding:
      1.) Indebtedness—Original amount of loan, date, principal amount, interest rate, monthly payment, current loan balance remaining, and number of payments.
      2.) Each investment—When purchased, adjusted tax basis, number of shares.
   g. Estate planning documents.

3. Analyzing and Evaluating the Client's Current Financial Status.

4. Developing the Recommendations.
   a. Should include cash flow projections.
   b. Should include a description of each goal and a plan and time frame for completion.

5. Communicating the Recommendations.

6. Implementing the Recommendations.

7. Monitoring the Recommendations

8. Practicing within Professional and Regulatory Standards (Throughout the Process).

Exhibit 2: Personal Financial Statements

1. Statement of Financial Position (Personal Balance Sheet).
   a. Assets and liabilities should be presented at fair market value.
   b. Statement needs to be appropriately dated.
   c. Net worth should be indicated.
   d. Footnotes should be utilized to describe details of both assets and liabilities.
   e. Property should be identified with owner (e.g., JTWROS, S1—individual ownership of the named spouse, and S2—individual ownership of the other named spouse).
   f. Asset categories.
      1.) Cash and cash equivalents.
      2.) Investments.
      3.) Personal use assets (residence, furniture, and autos).

g. Liabilities should be categorized according to maturity date.
   1.) Current liabilities—those due less than one year from the statement date.
   2.) Long-term liabilities—those due one year or more from the statement date.
h. Net worth = assets − liabilities.

2. Statement of Cash Flows
   a. Indicate period covered.
   b. Inflows:
      1.) Gross salaries.
      2.) Interest income.
      3.) Dividend income.
      4.) Rental income.
      5.) Refunds due (tax).
      6.) Other incoming cash flows.
      7.) Alimony received.
   c. Outflows:
      1.) Savings and investment—by item.
      2.) Fixed outflows—nondiscretionary.
         a.) House payments.
         b.) Auto payments.
         c.) Taxes.
      3.) Fixed outflows—discretionary. (club dues).
      4.) Variable outflows—nondiscretionary.
         a.) Food.
         b.) Utilities.
      5.) Variable outflows—discretionary.
         a.) Vacations.
         b.) Entertainment.
   d. Net cash flow = inflows − outflows (surplus or deficit).
   e. Footnotes should be used to explain.

Exhibit 3: Housing Costs and Debt Repayment

Indicators of Financial Strength and Weakness
As a Percentage of Gross Income

Type of Cost	Weak		Neutral	Strong	
	Extreme	Moderate		Moderate	Extreme
Housing Costs	≥40%	≥35%	≤30%	≤28%	≤20%
Housing Costs Plus Other Debt Repayments	≥48%	≥43%	≤38%	≤36%	≤28%

- Housing costs include principal payments, interest, taxes, insurance, and any association dues or costs.

- The total of all housing costs as a percentage of monthly gross income generally must be ≤28% to qualify for a mortgage.

- Other debt repayments include credit card payments, automobile loan payments, and student loan payments.

- The combination of housing costs and other monthly debt repayments generally must be ≤36% of monthly gross income to qualify for a home mortgage.

Exhibit 4: Annual Savings

As a Percentage of Annual Gross Income, by Age

Age, Years	Weak		Neutral	Strong	
	Extreme	Moderate		Moderate	Extreme
25	≤0%	≤2%	5%	≥7%	≥10%
30	≤0%	≤4%	7%	≥10%	≥13%
35	≤3%	≤7%	10%	≥13%	≥16%
40	≤6%	≤10%	13%	≥16%	≥19%
45	≤9%	≤13%	16%	≥19%	≥22%

This table assumes that the person is beginning a savings plan at the indicated age. Modification to the table will have to be made to accommodate analysis for a person who previously had some savings. This table is just a guide to wage replacement at about 80% of preretirement income, assuming a portfolio of 60% stocks and 40% fixed instruments.

Exhibit 5: Progress to Retirement, by Age and Income

An indicator of progress toward adequate retirement.
Assumes an 80% wage replacement ratio.

TARGET WEALTH LEVEL
Investment assets as a percentage of current income

INCOME LEVEL	$25,000 ▼
WAGE REPLACEMENT RATIO	80%
DISCOUNT RATE	9%

Inadequate Progress

Age, Years	VERY WEAK			WEAK		
	No SS	Single	WSAS	No SS	Single	WSAS
25	0.14	0.08	0.05	0.21	0.12	0.07
30	0.22	0.12	0.07	0.33	0.18	0.11
35	0.33	0.18	0.11	0.50	0.28	0.16
40	0.52	0.28	0.17	0.77	0.43	0.25
45	0.79	0.44	0.26	1.19	0.65	0.39
50	1.22	0.67	0.40	1.83	1.01	0.59
55	1.88	1.03	0.61	2.82	1.55	0.92
60	2.89	1.59	0.94	4.33	2.38	1.41
65	4.44	2.44	1.44	6.67	3.67	2.17

Adequate Progress

Age, Years	AVERAGE			GOOD		
	No SS	Single	WSAS	No SS	Single	WSAS
25	0.28	0.16	0.09	0.42	0.23	0.14
30	0.44	0.24	0.14	0.65	0.36	0.21
35	0.67	0.37	0.22	1.00	0.55	0.33
40	1.03	0.57	0.34	1.55	0.85	0.50
45	1.59	0.87	0.52	2.38	1.31	0.77
50	2.44	1.34	0.79	3.66	2.01	1.19
55	3.75	2.07	1.22	5.63	3.10	1.83
60	5.78	3.18	1.88	8.67	4.77	2.82
65	8.89	4.89	2.89	13.33	7.33	4.33

Strong Progress

Age, Years	STRONG			EXTRA STRONG		
	No SS	Single	WSAS	No SS	Single	WSAS
25	0.71	0.39	0.23	0.99	0.54	0.32
30	1.09	0.60	0.35	1.52	0.84	0.50
35	1.67	0.92	0.54	2.34	1.29	0.76
40	2.58	1.42	0.84	3.61	1.98	1.17
45	3.97	2.18	1.29	5.55	3.05	1.80
50	6.10	3.36	1.98	8.54	4.70	2.78
55	9.39	5.16	3.05	13.14	7.23	4.27
60	14.44	7.94	4.69	20.22	11.12	6.57
65	22.22	12.22	7.22	31.11	17.11	10.11

No SS = No Social Security   Single = Social Security benefits for a single person
WSAS = Social Security benefits for a married individual whose spouse is not working and is the same age

Exhibit 5: Progress to Retirement, by Age and Income (*continued*)

TARGET WEALTH LEVEL
Investment assets as a percentage of current income

INCOME LEVEL	$40,000 ▼
WAGE REPLACEMENT RATIO	80%
DISCOUNT RATE	9%

Inadequate Progress

Age, Years	VERY WEAK			VERY WEAK		
	No SS	Single	WSAS	No SS	Single	WSAS
25	0.14	0.09	0.06	0.21	0.13	0.09
30	0.22	0.14	0.10	0.33	0.20	0.14
35	0.33	0.21	0.15	0.50	0.31	0.22
40	0.52	0.32	0.23	0.77	0.48	0.34
45	0.79	0.50	0.35	1.19	0.74	0.52
50	1.22	0.76	0.53	1.83	1.14	0.80
55	1.88	1.17	0.82	2.82	1.76	1.23
60	2.89	1.81	1.26	4.33	2.71	1.90
65	4.44	2.78	1.94	6.67	4.17	2.92

Adequate Progress

Age, Years	AVERAGE			GOOD		
	No SS	Single	WSAS	No SS	Single	WSAS
25	0.28	0.18	0.12	0.42	0.27	0.19
30	0.44	0.27	0.19	0.65	0.41	0.29
35	0.67	0.42	0.29	1.00	0.63	0.44
40	1.03	0.64	0.45	1.55	0.97	0.68
45	1.59	0.99	0.69	2.38	1.49	1.04
50	2.44	1.53	1.07	3.66	2.29	1.60
55	3.75	2.35	1.64	5.63	3.52	2.46
60	5.78	3.61	2.53	8.67	5.42	3.79
65	8.89	5.56	3.89	13.33	8.33	5.83

Strong Progress

Age, Years	STRONG			EXTRA STRONG		
	No SS	Single	WSAS	No SS	Single	WSAS
25	0.71	0.44	0.31	0.99	0.62	0.43
30	1.09	0.68	0.48	1.52	0.95	0.67
35	1.67	1.05	0.73	2.34	1.47	1.03
40	2.58	1.61	1.13	3.61	2.25	1.58
45	3.97	2.48	1.73	5.55	3.47	2.43
50	6.10	3.81	2.67	8.54	5.34	3.74
55	9.39	5.87	4.11	13.14	8.21	5.75
60	14.44	9.03	6.32	20.22	12.64	8.85
65	22.22	13.89	9.72	31.11	19.44	13.61

Exhibit 5: Progress to Retirement, by Age and Income (*continued*)

TARGET WEALTH LEVEL
Investment assets as a percentage of current income

INCOME LEVEL	$55,000 ▼
WAGE REPLACEMENT RATIO	80%
DISCOUNT RATE	9%

Inadequate Progress

Age, Years	VERY WEAK			WEAK		
	No SS	Single	WSAS	No SS	Single	WSAS
25	0.14	0.10	0.08	0.21	0.15	0.11
30	0.22	0.15	0.12	0.33	0.23	0.18
35	0.33	0.23	0.18	0.50	0.35	0.27
40	0.52	0.36	0.28	0.77	0.54	0.42
45	0.79	0.55	0.43	1.19	0.82	0.64
50	1.22	0.85	0.66	1.83	1.27	0.99
55	1.88	1.30	1.01	2.82	1.95	1.52
60	2.89	2.00	1.56	4.33	3.00	2.34
65	4.44	3.08	2.40	6.67	4.62	3.60

Adequate Progress

Age, Years	AVERAGE			GOOD		
	No SS	Single	WSAS	No SS	Single	WSAS
25	0.28	0.20	0.15	0.42	0.29	0.23
30	0.44	0.30	0.24	0.65	0.45	0.35
35	0.67	0.46	0.36	1.00	0.70	0.54
40	1.03	0.71	0.56	1.55	1.07	0.83
45	1.59	1.10	0.86	2.38	1.65	1.28
50	2.44	1.69	1.32	3.66	2.54	1.98
55	3.75	2.60	2.03	5.63	3.90	3.04
60	5.78	4.00	3.12	8.67	6.01	4.68
65	8.89	6.16	4.80	13.33	9.24	7.20

Strong Progress

Age, Years	STRONG			EXTRA STRONG		
	No SS	Single	WSAS	No SS	Single	WSAS
25	0.71	0.49	0.38	0.99	0.69	0.53
30	1.09	0.75	0.59	1.52	1.06	0.82
35	1.67	1.16	0.90	2.34	1.63	1.27
40	2.58	1.79	1.39	3.61	2.50	1.95
45	3.97	2.75	2.14	5.55	3.85	3.00
50	6.10	4.23	3.29	8.54	5.92	4.61
55	9.39	6.51	5.07	13.14	9.11	7.09
60	14.44	10.01	7.80	20.22	14.02	10.91
65	22.22	15.40	11.99	31.11	21.57	16.79

Exhibit 5: Progress to Retirement, by Age and Income (*continued*)

TARGET WEALTH LEVEL
Investment assets as a percentage of current income

INCOME LEVEL	$70,000 ▼
WAGE REPLACEMENT RATIO	80%
DISCOUNT RATE	9%

Inadequate Progress

Age, Years	VERY WEAK			WEAK		
	No SS	Single	WSAS	No SS	Single	WSAS
25	0.14	0.11	0.09	0.21	0.16	0.13
30	0.22	0.16	0.14	0.33	0.24	0.20
35	0.33	0.25	0.21	0.50	0.38	0.31
40	0.52	0.39	0.32	0.77	0.58	0.48
45	0.79	0.59	0.50	1.19	0.89	0.74
50	1.22	0.92	0.76	1.83	1.37	1.14
55	1.88	1.41	1.17	2.82	2.11	1.76
60	2.89	2.17	1.81	4.33	3.25	2.71
65	4.44	3.33	2.78	6.67	5.00	4.17

Adequate Progress

Age, Years	AVERAGE			GOOD		
	No SS	Single	WSAS	No SS	Single	WSAS
25	0.28	0.21	0.18	0.42	0.32	0.27
30	0.44	0.33	0.27	0.65	0.49	0.41
35	0.67	0.50	0.42	1.00	0.75	0.63
40	1.03	0.77	0.64	1.55	1.16	0.97
45	1.59	1.19	0.99	2.38	1.78	1.49
50	2.44	1.83	1.53	3.66	2.75	2.29
55	3.75	2.82	2.35	5.63	4.22	3.52
60	5.78	4.33	3.61	8.67	6.50	5.42
65	8.89	6.67	5.56	13.33	10.00	8.33

Strong Progress

Age, Years	STRONG			EXTRA STRONG		
	No SS	Single	WSAS	No SS	Single	WSAS
25	0.71	0.53	0.44	0.99	0.74	0.62
30	1.09	0.82	0.68	1.52	1.14	0.95
35	1.67	1.26	1.05	2.34	1.76	1.47
40	2.58	1.93	1.61	3.61	2.71	2.25
45	3.97	2.97	2.48	5.55	4.16	3.47
50	6.10	4.58	3.81	8.54	6.41	5.34
55	9.39	7.04	5.87	13.14	9.86	8.21
60	14.44	10.83	9.03	20.22	15.17	12.64
65	22.22	16.67	13.89	31.11	23.33	19.44

Exhibit 5: Progress to Retirement, by Age and Income (*continued*)

TARGET WEALTH LEVEL		
Investment assets as a percentage of current income		

INCOME LEVEL		$85,000 ▼
WAGE REPLACEMENT RATIO		80%
DISCOUNT RATE		9%

Inadequate Progress

Age, Years	VERY WEAK			WEAK		
	No SS	Single	WSAS	No SS	Single	WSAS
25	0.14	0.11	0.10	0.21	0.17	0.15
30	0.22	0.17	0.15	0.33	0.26	0.23
35	0.33	0.27	0.23	0.50	0.40	0.35
40	0.52	0.41	0.36	0.77	0.61	0.53
45	0.79	0.63	0.55	1.19	0.94	0.82
50	1.22	0.97	0.84	1.83	1.45	1.27
55	1.88	1.49	1.30	2.82	2.24	1.95
60	2.89	2.29	2.00	4.33	3.44	2.99
65	4.44	3.53	3.07	6.67	5.29	4.61

Adequate Progress

Age, Years	AVERAGE			GOOD		
	No SS	Single	WSAS	No SS	Single	WSAS
25	0.28	0.22	0.20	0.42	0.34	0.29
30	0.44	0.35	0.30	0.65	0.52	0.45
35	0.67	0.53	0.46	1.00	0.80	0.69
40	1.03	0.82	0.71	1.55	1.23	1.07
45	1.59	1.26	1.10	2.38	1.89	1.64
50	2.44	1.94	1.69	3.66	2.91	2.53
55	3.75	2.98	2.60	5.63	4.47	3.89
60	5.78	4.59	3.99	8.67	6.88	5.99
65	8.89	7.06	6.14	13.33	10.59	9.22

Strong Progress

Age, Years	STRONG			EXTRA STRONG		
	No SS	Single	WSAS	No SS	Single	WSAS
25	0.71	0.56	0.49	0.99	0.79	0.68
30	1.09	0.86	0.75	1.52	1.21	1.05
35	1.67	1.33	1.16	2.34	1.86	1.62
40	2.58	2.05	1.78	3.61	2.87	2.49
45	3.97	3.15	2.74	5.55	4.41	3.84
50	6.10	4.84	4.22	8.54	6.78	5.90
55	9.39	7.45	6.49	13.14	10.44	9.08
60	14.44	11.47	9.98	20.22	16.06	13.98
65	22.22	17.65	15.36	31.11	24.71	21.50

Exhibit 5: Progress to Retirement, by Age and Income (*continued*)

TARGET WEALTH LEVEL
Investment assets as a percentage of current income

INCOME LEVEL	$100,000 ▼
WAGE REPLACEMENT RATIO	80%
DISCOUNT RATE	9%

Inadequate Progress

Age, Years	VERY WEAK			WEAK		
	No SS	Single	WSAS	No SS	Single	WSAS
25	0.14	0.12	0.10	0.21	0.18	0.16
30	0.22	0.18	0.16	0.33	0.27	0.24
35	0.33	0.28	0.25	0.50	0.41	0.37
40	0.52	0.43	0.38	0.77	0.64	0.57
45	0.79	0.65	0.58	1.19	0.98	0.88
50	1.22	1.01	0.90	1.83	1.51	1.35
55	1.88	1.55	1.38	2.82	2.32	2.08
60	2.89	2.38	2.13	4.33	3.57	3.20
65	4.44	3.67	3.28	6.67	5.50	4.92

Adequate Progress

Age, Years	AVERAGE			GOOD		
	No SS	Single	WSAS	No SS	Single	WSAS
25	0.28	0.23	0.21	0.42	0.35	0.31
30	0.44	0.36	0.32	0.65	0.54	0.48
35	0.67	0.55	0.49	1.00	0.83	0.74
40	1.03	0.85	0.76	1.55	1.28	1.14
45	1.59	1.31	1.17	2.38	1.96	1.75
50	2.44	2.01	1.80	3.66	3.02	2.70
55	3.75	3.10	2.77	5.63	4.65	4.15
60	5.78	4.77	4.26	8.67	7.15	6.39
65	8.89	7.33	6.56	13.33	11.00	9.83

Strong Progress

Age, Years	STRONG			EXTRA STRONG		
	No SS	Single	WSAS	No SS	Single	WSAS
25	0.71	0.58	0.52	0.99	0.82	0.73
30	1.09	0.90	0.80	1.52	1.26	1.12
35	1.67	1.38	1.24	2.34	1.93	1.73
40	2.58	2.13	1.90	3.61	2.98	2.66
45	3.97	3.27	2.92	5.55	4.58	4.09
50	6.10	5.03	4.50	8.54	7.05	6.30
55	9.39	7.74	6.92	13.14	10.84	9.69
60	14.44	11.92	10.65	20.22	16.68	14.91
65	22.22	18.33	16.39	31.11	25.67	22.94

Exhibit 6: Typical Strengths and Weaknesses

Strengths	Weaknesses
Adequate savings	Insufficient savings
Valid and current estate planning documents	Lack of estate planning documents
Appropriate use of debt	Inappropriate debt use
Appropriate investments given client risk tolerance	Inappropriate investments given client risk tolerance
Appropriate risk coverage	Insufficient amount of or no risk coverage
Appropriate net worth given client goals	Low net worth given client goals
Appropriate emergency fund	Inadequate emergency fund
Well-defined financial goals	Financial goals that are not defined or unrealistic
Excellent cash flow management skills (including proper debt management)	Poor or improper cash flow management skills
Employment status stable or promising	Unfavorable employment status

Exhibit 7: Summary of Various Company Ratings

Rank	AM Best	Best's Description	Fitch[1]	Moody's[2]	S&P[3]
1	A++	Superior	AAA	Aaa	AAA
2	A+	Superior	AA	Aa	AA
3	A	Excellent	A	A	A
4	A−	Excellent	BBB	Baa	BBB
5	B++	Good	BB	Ba	BBB−
6	B+	Good	B	B	BB+
7	B	Fair	CCC	Caa	BB
8	B−	Fair	CC	Ca	B
9	C++	Marginal	C	C	CCC
10	C+	Marginal	RD		CC
11	C	Weak	D		C
12	C−	Weak			D
13	D	Poor			
14	E	Under Regulatory Supervision			
15	F	In Liquidation			
16	S	Suspended			

[1] International Issuer and Credit Rating Scales
[2] Global Long-Term Rating Scale
[3] Global Rating Scale

Exhibit 8: Life Insurance Policy Replacement

The decision to replace one policy with another should be made cautiously. The methodology for such a decision includes fact gathering, calculations, and benchmark comparisons.

The Belth price of protection model formula is as follows:

$$CPT = \frac{(P + CV_0)(1 + i) - (CV_1 + D)}{(DB - CV_1)(0.001)}$$

CPT	=	cost (price of protection)
P	=	annual premium
CV_0	=	cash value at beginning of year
i	=	net after tax earning rate
CV_1	=	cash value at year-end
D	=	current dividend
DB	=	death benefit

Compare to benchmark table:

- If cost is less than the benchmark price, then retain the policy.

- If cost is greater than the benchmark but less than 2 times the benchmark, then retain the policy.

- If cost is greater than 2 times the benchmark, consider replacement.

Table (Joseph M. Belth, author)

Age, Years	Benchmark Price of Insurance per $1,000
<30	$1.50
30–34	$2.00
35–39	$3.00
40–44	$4.00
45–49	$6.50
50–54	$10.00
55–59	$15.00
60–64	$25.00
65–69	$35.00
70–74	$50.00
75–79	$80.00
80–84	$125.00

Exhibit 9: Summary of Homeowners Insurance Policies

There are six standard homeowners policy forms.

HO-2: broad form, residential. This named-peril form policy insures the dwelling, other structures, and personal property for specifically named perils.

HO-3: special form, residential. This special form insures the dwelling and other property against losses to the property for open perils (all except those specifically excluded). Personal property is subject to the same named-peril coverage as HO-2 (unless an endorsement is added).

HO-4: contents broad form, residential, and tenant. HO-4 provides protection from named perils (same as HO-2) for a tenant's personal property.

HO-5: comprehensive form, residential. The HO-5 is similar to HO-3 except the coverage for personal property. HO-3 covers personal property on a broad perils basis. HO-5, however, covers personal property on an open-perils basis.

HO-6: unit-owners form, condominium. HO-6 insures the personal property of the insured (condominium owner) for named perils (same perils as HO-2).

HO-8: modified coverage form, residential. This modified coverage provides protection for dwellings that have a fair market value (FMV) that is less than the replacement value of the dwelling (for example: a home, actual cash value of $150,000 with a replacement value of $400,000).

Exhibit 10: List of Covered Perils

BASIC NAMED PERILS		
1. Fire	5. Riot or civil commotion	9. Vandalism or malicious mischief
2. Lightning	6. Aircraft	10. Explosion
3. Windstorm	7. Vehicles	11. Theft
4. Hail	8. Smoke	12. Volcanic eruption

BROAD NAMED PERILS

Basic Named Perils 1–12, plus 13–18

13. Falling objects

14. Weight of ice, snow, or sleet

15. Accidental discharge or overflow of water or stream

16. Sudden and accidental tearing apart, cracking, burning, or bulging of a steam, hot water, air conditioning, or automatic fire protective sprinkler system, or from within a household appliance

17. Freezing of a plumbing, heating, air conditioning, or automatic fire sprinkler system, or of a household appliance

18. Sudden and accidental damage from artificially generated electrical current

	HO-2	HO-3	HO-4	HO-5	HO-6	HO-8
Coverage A—Dwelling	Broad	Open	N/A	Open	Limited	Basic
Coverage B—Other Structures	Broad	Open	N/A	Open	N/A	Basic
Coverage C—Personal Property	Broad	Broad*	Broad	Open	Broad	Basic
Coverage D—Loss of Use	Broad	Open	Broad	Open	Broad	Basic

*Can be endorsed with HO-15 endorsement to provide coverage for personal property on an open perils basis and can be endorsed to provide loss settlement for personal property on a replacement cost basis.

Exhibit 11: Eight General Exclusions for Homeowners

- ◼ Ordinance or Law
- ◼ Earth Movement
- ◼ Water Damage
- ◼ Power Failure

- ◼ Neglect
- ◼ War
- ◼ Nuclear Hazard
- ◼ Intentional Loss

Exhibit 12: Group Term Life Insurance Cost Per $1,000 of Protection for One Month (IRC §79)

Age, Years	Monthly Cost per $1,000
<25	$0.05
25–29	$0.06
30–34	$0.08
35–39	$0.09
40–44	$0.10
45–49	$0.15
50–54	$0.23
55–59	$0.43
60–64	$0.66
65–69	$1.27
≥70	$2.06

Exhibit 13: Total Risk

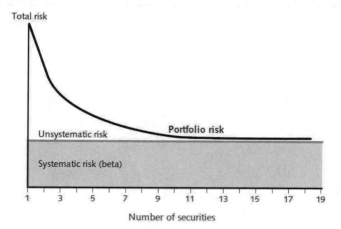

Exhibit 14: Systematic and Unsystematic Risks

Systematic Risks	Unsystematic Risks
Purchasing Power Risk	Business Risk
Reinvestment Rate Risk	Financial Risk
Interest Rate Risk	Default Risk
Market Risk	Political Risk
Exchange Rate Risk	Tax Risk
	Investment Manager Risk

Exhibit 15: Risk Pyramid

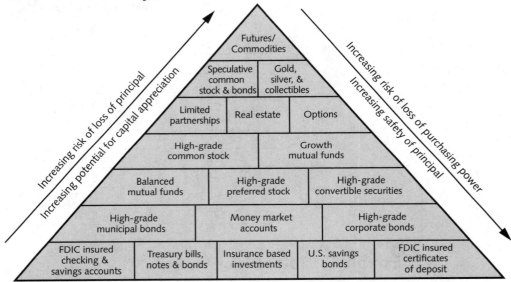

Exhibit 16: Summary of Rates of Return for Various Securities

Type of Security	Rate of Return	Standard Deviation (σ)
Small Cap. Stocks	12%	35%
Large Cap. Stocks	10%	21%
Corporate Bonds	5%	9%
Intermediate Govt. Bonds	5%	9%
Long-Term Govt. Bonds	5%	9%
Treasury Bills	4%	3%
Inflation	3%	5%

The previous table depicts the approximate performance and risk level of various securities over a 50-year time period. Notice that the bonds have hardly outpaced the rate of inflation over this long period of time. Stocks have performed substantially better than bonds over the same period of time; however, stocks have sustained substantially more volatility than bonds. The investors who have long-term perspectives and are willing to sustain higher levels of volatility are more suited to equity-type investments.

Exhibit 17: The Call Option

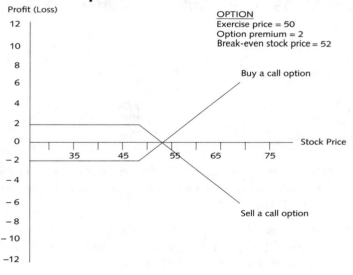

The exhibit above depicts the profit (loss) for both a buyer and a seller of a call option. Notice that the buyer has unlimited profit potential, whereas the seller has unlimited loss potential. Likewise, the buyer's loss and the seller's gain are limited to the premium paid.

Exhibit 18: The Put Option

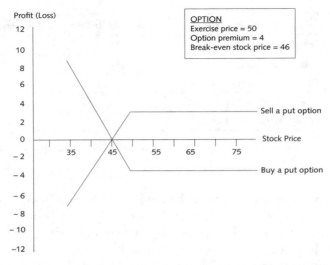

The exhibit above depicts the profit (loss) for both a buyer and a seller of a put option. Notice that the buyer has a large profit potential, whereas the seller has a large loss potential. Likewise, the buyer's loss and the seller's gain are limited to the premium paid.

Exhibit 19: Area Under the Curve

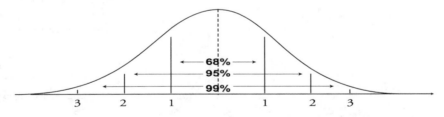

■ The curve represents 100% of possible outcomes. These outcomes tend to cluster around the mean; however, some occurrences will fall away from the mean (i.e., in the tails of the bell-shaped curve).

■ Approximately 68% of outcomes will fall within one standard deviation (both above and below) of the mean. **Note:** One standard deviation will be different for each individual security and may have a wide range.

■ Approximately 95% of outcomes will fall within two standard deviations (both above and below) of the mean.

■ Approximately 99% of outcomes will fall within three standard deviations (both above and below) of the mean.

■ This information about the normal curve allows investors to determine the probability of specific outcomes.

Exhibit 20: Standard Deviation of Two Securities

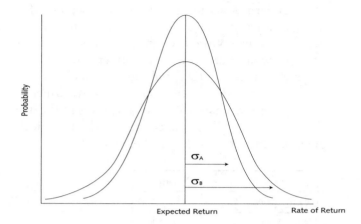

The exhibit above illustrates that two securities can have the same expected return with different levels of risk. Security B is more risky than Security A because its standard deviation is greater.

Exhibit 21: Explanation of Standard Deviation and Expected Return

Standard deviation is an absolute measure of the variability of the actual investment returns around the average or mean of those returns (otherwise known as the expected return of the investment). This measure is the single most accepted measure of total, or absolute, risk in investment theory and tells an investor how far from the mean the investment's actual return is likely to vary.

The standard deviation for a set of investment returns can be calculated very efficiently using a financial calculator, such as the HP 10BII. Using the information in the first column of the table below as the historical returns over a 12-year period for a given investment, the keystrokes would be:

Keystrokes	Display
[■] [C] [ALL}	0.0000
13.5 [Σ+]	1.0000
12.0 [Σ+]	2.0000
5.0 [Σ+]	3.0000
± 2.0 [Σ+]	4.0000
7.0 [Σ+]	5.0000
23.0 [Σ+]	6.0000
6.0 [Σ+]	7.0000
10.0 [Σ+]	8.0000
45.0 [Σ+]	9.0000
10.0 [Σ+]	10.0000
0.5 [Σ+]	11.0000
14.0 [Σ+]	12.0000
[■][SxSy]	12.2938

Expected return is the return the investor demands or expects to make and is computed by multiplying each of the investment's possible annual returns by the probability that they will occur and adding the results. For example, the following observations: 9, 11, 13, with the following probabilities: 0.25, 0.50, 0.25, will yield an expected return of 11. This figure is calculated as follows: $(0.25 \times 9) + (0.50 \times 11) + (0.25 \times 13) = 11$.

Exhibit 22: Performance Measurements

1. **Holding Period Return (HPR).**

   a. The holding period return is the basic method used to evaluate the speed at which an investment grows or declines. This return is determined by dividing the change in wealth by the initial investment.

   b. The formula for the holding period return is as follows:

   $$\frac{\text{ending value (EV)} - \text{beginning value (BV)} \pm \text{cash flows (CF)}}{\text{beginning value (BV)}}$$

   c. The holding period return refers to the overall percentage gain the investor has received. The holding period return is not often used as a measure of performance because it ignores the time value of money, and it does not address the time over which the investment has grown.

2. **Arithmetic Mean.**

   a. The arithmetic mean, which is the same as a normal average or mean, is equal to the sum of the returns per interval divided by the number of observations. For example, the mean for the following set of data would be approximately 12.41%.

Yr 1	Yr 2	Yr 3	Yr 4	Yr 5	Yr 6	Yr 7	Yr 8
12.1%	10.0%	11.3%	15.2%	9.1%	6.5%	18.3%	16.8%

   b. The arithmetic mean is an approximation of the earnings rate for an investment over time; however, large fluctuations in returns from year to year, especially negative returns, will have a tendency to cause the arithmetic mean to be inaccurate.

3. **Geometric Mean.**

   a. Geometric mean is the average compounded return, or the internal rate of return (annualized return). This mean is calculated by subtracting 1 from the 1/nth root of the product of each interval return plus 1. Therefore, the geometric mean for the data above is equal to $[(1 + 0.121) \times (1 + 0.100) \times (1 + 0.113) \times (1 + 0.152) \times (1 + 0.091) \times (1 + 0.065) \times (1 + 0.183) \times (1 + 0.168)]^{1/8} - 1$. Thus, the compound annual return is equal to 12.35%.

   b. The arithmetic and geometric means are different because the arithmetic mean does not take into consideration the compounding effect of the returns.

4. **Real Return (inflation adjusted).**

   a. The loss of purchasing power is one of the risks that investors face in achieving their financial goals. Real returns reflect the excess earnings from an investment that are above the inflation rate. Simply subtracting the rate of inflation from the investment rate of return, however, will not yield the real return.

b. The real return can be calculated using the following formula:

$$\left[\frac{(1+\text{nominal return})}{(1+\text{inflation rate})}-1\right]\times100$$

5. **Total Return.**
   a. The total return for any investment can be thought of as the sum of the appreciation and the earnings from that investment. For example, a typical annual dividend paid (income or earnings) on a stock is 2%. If, in addition, the market value of the stock increases 6% from the beginning of the year to year end, the investor would have a total return on the stock of 8% (2% income + 6% capital appreciation).

6. **Internal Rate of Return (IRR).**
   a. The IRR is the earnings rate at which the present value of a series of cash flows will equal its cost.

$$P_0 = \frac{CF_1}{(1+r)^1} + \frac{CF_2}{(1+r)^2} + \cdots + \frac{CF_t}{(1+r)^t}$$

P_0 = the value of the security today
CF_t = the cash flow for period t
r = the discount rate or internal rate of return
t = the number of cash flows to be evaluated

   b. The underlying assumption of this equation is that the cash flows that occur during the life of the investment will be reinvested at the investment's internal rate of return. This is the same assumption found in computing the yield to maturity.

7. **Time-Weighted Return versus Dollar-Weighted Return.**

A time-weighted return is determined without regard to any subsequent cash flows of the investor. As such, it measures the performance of the investment over a period of time (and not of the investor as in a dollar-weighted approach). Most returns reported on mutual funds are time-weighted because the portfolio manager does not have any control over the future cash flows to the fund with respect to investor dollars.

In contrast, a dollar-weighted return considers subsequent contributions to and withdrawals from an investment, including sales of, for example, stock. As a result, the dollar-weighted approach focuses on the return of the investor (not the investment, as in the time-weighted approach) over a period of time, and usually results in a rate of return different than the time-weighted method.

8. **Tax-Adjusted Returns.**

   A tax-adjusted return is the realized return multiplied by (1 − tax rate). Taxes should be factored in when comparing one investment alternative to another. For example, the after-tax yield on a municipal bond may be higher than for a corporate bond, even though the corporate bond carries a higher stated rate of return or has a higher yield to maturity. The after-tax return should reflect both federal and local taxes.

   Nontaxable Income.

   a. Federal—The interest from municipal bonds is not taxable by the federal government. In addition, unrealized appreciation is not taxable by the federal government.

   b. Municipalities—The interest from Treasury bills, bonds, and notes, as well as from savings bonds, is not taxable by states and municipalities. Additionally, most municipalities do not tax interest from municipal bonds issued by their own government.

9. **Risk-Adjusted Returns.**

   Benchmark returns should be compared against some standard, such as the S&P 500 Index. As mentioned above, comparing after-tax returns of different investments is important in investment planning. Another comparison is the risk-adjusted return. Knowing that the return from an investment is not only better than a more conservative investment but is also better on a risk-adjusted basis is important. This permits the investor to determine whether the return was worth the risk that was undertaken.

   Treynor, Sharpe, and Jensen performance measures are possible methods of comparing risk-adjusted returns.

10. **Weighted-Average Return.**

    The weighted-average return represents the return for a set of securities, such as a portfolio, where each return is weighted by the proportion of the security to the entire group or portfolio.

Exhibit 23: Investment Formulas

Security Market Line (SML)

$$r_s = r_f + (r_m - r_f)\, \beta_\iota$$

r_s = portfolio expected return

r_f = risk-free rate of return

r_m = market rate of return

β_ι = beta, measures the systematic risk associated with a particular portfolio

$(r_m - r_f)$ = market risk premium (the return from the market that exceeds the risk-free rate of return)

$(r_m - r_f)\, \beta_i$ = stock risk premium

Arbitrage Pricing Theory (APT)

Arbitrage pricing theory (APT)

$$r_i = a_0 + b_1 F_1 + b_2 F_2 + \ldots + b_n F_n + e$$

r_i = expected return from the security

a_0 = risk-free rate of return

b_n = sensitivity of the security to factor F_n

F_n = factor that affects the security

e = return that is unique to the security (error term)

Note: The error term should drop out if all relevant factors are captured by the equation.

Measures of Risk

Weighted-average beta

$$\beta_w = \sum_{i=1}^{n} (\beta_i \times \%_i)$$

β_w = weighted-average beta

β_i = beta return for security i

$\%_i$ = portion of security i to total portfolio

n = number of securities

Expected rate of return

$$E(r) = P_1(r_1) + P_2(r_2) + \dots + P_t(r_t)$$

$E(r)$ = expected return

P_1 = probability assigned to the first rate of return

r_1 = first rate of return

t = number of events being examined

Standard deviation of forecasted returns

$$\sigma = \{P_1[r_1 - E(r)]^2 + P_2[r_2 - E(r)]^2 + \dots + P_t[r_t - E(r)]^2\}^{\frac{1}{2}}$$

$E(r)$ = expected return (calculated)

r_t = forecasted return for outcome t

P_t = probability of outcome t

Financial Ratios

Liquidity Ratios

Current ratio	$\dfrac{\text{Current assets}}{\text{Current liabilities}}$
Acid test or quick ratio	$\dfrac{\text{Current assets} - \text{inventory}}{\text{Current liabilities}}$

Activity Ratios

Inventory turnover ratio	$\dfrac{\text{Cost of goods sold}}{\text{Average inventory}}$
Accounts receivable turnover	$\dfrac{\text{Sales}}{\text{Average accounts receivable}}$
Fixed asset turnover	$\dfrac{\text{Annual sales}}{\text{Fixed assets}}$

Profitability Ratios

Operating profit margin	$\dfrac{\text{Earnings before interest and taxes}}{\text{Sales}}$
Net profit margin	$\dfrac{\text{Net income}}{\text{Sales}}$
Return on assets (ROA)	$\dfrac{\text{Net income}}{\text{Total assets}}$
Return on equity (ROE)	$\dfrac{\text{Net income}}{\text{Equity}}$

Debt Ratios

Debt ratio	$\dfrac{\text{Total debt}}{\text{Total assets}}$
Debt-equity ratio	$\dfrac{\text{Total debt}}{\text{Total equity}}$

Ratios for Bond Analysis*

Times interest earned	$\dfrac{\text{Earnings before interest and taxes}}{\text{Annual interest charges}}$

*Also see inventory turnover and accounts receivables turnover

Ratios for Stock Analysis**

Dividend payout ratio	$\dfrac{\text{Dividends}}{\text{Earnings}}$
Price-to-earnings ratio (basic calculation)	$\dfrac{\text{Market price per share}}{\text{Earnings per share}}$

**Also see ROE, ROA, and net profit margin

Rates of Return

Holding period return (HPR)

$$HPR = \frac{\text{ending value of investment} - \text{beginning value of investment} +/- \text{cash flows}}{\text{beginning value of investment}}$$

Internal rate of return (IRR)

$$PV = \frac{CF_1}{(1 + y)^1} + \frac{CF_2}{(1 + y)^2} + \ldots + \frac{CF_t}{(1 + y)^t}$$

PV = present value of the security

CF_t = cash flow for a particular period

y = the internal rate of return (discount rate or earnings rate)

t = number of cash flows to be evaluated

Yield to maturity (YTM)

$$PV = \frac{CF_1}{(1 + y)^1} + \frac{CF_2}{(1 + y)^2} + \ldots + \frac{\text{par value}}{(1 + y)^t}$$

PV = present value of the security

CF_t = cash flow for a particular period

y = discount rate per period—yield to maturity

t = number of cash flows to be evaluated

Yield to call (YTC)

$$PV = \frac{CF_1}{(1 + y)^1} + \frac{CF_2}{(1 + y)^2} + \ldots + \frac{\text{call price}}{(1 + y)^t}$$

PV = present value of the security

CF_t = cash flow for period t

y = discount rate per period—yield to call

t = number of periods until the call date

Arithmetic mean

$$AM = \frac{\sum_{t=1}^{n} HPR_t}{n}$$

Geometric mean

$$\text{geometric mean} = \sqrt[n]{(1+r_1)(1+r_2)(1+r_3)\ldots(1+r_n)} - 1$$

r_n = return for each period

n = number of periods

After-tax rate of return

Tax-adjusted return = $R(1 - TR)$

R = before-tax return or earnings rate

TR = tax rate

Real return (inflation adjusted)

$$\left[\frac{(1+R_n)}{(1+I)} - 1 \right] \times 100$$

R_n = absolute return

I = rate of inflation for the period

Weighted-average return

$$\overline{X_w} = \sum_{i=1}^{N} [(R_i)(\%_i)]$$

$\overline{X_w}$ = weighted average

R_i = return for security i

$\%_i$ = portion of security i to total portfolio

N = number of securities

Valuation Models

Basic present value model

$$PV = \frac{CF_1}{(1+y)^1} + \frac{CF_2}{(1+y)^2} + \ldots + \frac{CF_t}{(1+y)^t}$$

PV = present value of the security

CF_t = cash flow for a particular period

y = discount rate based on the type of security and risk level of the investment

t = number of cash flows to be evaluated

Discounted Free Cash Flow Model

$$V = \frac{FCFE_1}{r-g} = \frac{FCFE_0 \times (1+g)}{r-g}$$

V = intrinsic value

$FCFE_0$ = free cash flow to equity in current year

$FCFE_1$ = free cash flow to equity in period 1

r = required rate of return

g = growth rate

Capitalized earnings

$$V = \frac{E}{R_D}$$

V = estimated value of the company or firm

E = earnings for the company or firm

R_D = discount (capitalization) rate

Perpetuity

$$V = \frac{D_1}{r}$$

V = intrinsic value of the stock

D_1 = dividend paid at the end of period 1

r = investor's required rate of return

* Conversion Value

$$CV = \frac{Par}{CP} \times P_s$$

CV = conversion value

CP = conversion price of the security

P_s = current market price of the security

Note: Par = $1,000, CV is also used to denote Coefficient of Variation.

Exhibit 24: Formula Page Provided on CFP® Certification Exam

(The formula sheet below was current at press time. Please refer to **http://www.cfp.net/Upload/Publications/170.pdf** for any subsequent updates to the formula sheet.)

Provided Formulas

These formulas are available to exam candidates when taking the CFP® Certification Examination:

$$V = \frac{D_1}{r - g}$$

$$r = \frac{D_1}{P} + g$$

$$COV_{ij} = \rho_{ij}\sigma_i\sigma_j$$

$$\sigma_p = \sqrt{W_i^2\sigma_i^2 + W_j^2\sigma_j^2 + 2W_iW_jCOV_{ij}}$$

$$\beta_i = \frac{COV_{im}}{\sigma_m^2} = \frac{\rho_{im}\sigma_i}{\sigma_m}$$

$$\sigma_r = \sqrt{\frac{\sum_{t=1}^{n}(r_t - \bar{r})^2}{n}}$$

$$S_r = \sqrt{\frac{\sum_{t=1}^{n}(r_t - \bar{r})^2}{n-1}}$$

$$r_i = r_f + (r_m - r_f)\beta_i$$

$$\alpha_p = \bar{r}_p - \left[\bar{r}_f + \left(\bar{r}_m - \bar{r}_f\right)\beta_p\right]$$

$$T_p = \frac{\bar{r}_p - \bar{r}_f}{\beta_p}$$

$$D = \frac{1+y}{y} - \frac{(1+y)+t(c-y)}{c\left[(1+y)^t - 1\right] + y}$$

$$\frac{\Delta P}{P} = -D\left[\frac{\Delta y}{1+y}\right]$$

$$IR = \frac{R_P - R_B}{\sigma_A}$$

$$EAR = \left(1 + \frac{i}{n}\right)^n - 1$$

$$TEY = r/(1-t)$$

$$AM = \frac{a_1 + a_2 + a_3 + \cdots + a_n}{n}$$

$$S_p = \frac{\bar{r}_p - \bar{r}_f}{\sigma_p}$$

$$_1R_N = [(1 + _1R_1)\,(1 + E(_2r_1))\ldots(1 + E(_Nr_1))]^{1/N} -$$

$$HPR = [(1+r_1) \times (1+r_2) \times \ldots(1+r_n)] - 1$$

$$\sqrt[n]{(1+r_1) \times (1+r_2) \times \ldots(1+r_n)} - 1$$

Reprinted, with permission, from the CFP Board's *Guide to CFP® Certification*.

Exhibit 25: Tax-Rate Schedules (2016 and 2017)

2016 TAX RATES AND BRACKETS

Single – Schedule X			
If Taxable Income Is: Over—	**But Not Over—**	**The Tax Is:**	**Of the Amount Over—**
$0	$9,275	$0 + 10%	$0
9,275	37,650	927.50 + 15%	9,275
37,650	91,150	5,183.75 + 25%	37,650
91,150	190,150	18,558.75 + 28%	91,150
190,150	413,350	46,278.75 + 33%	190,150
413,350	$415,050	119,934.75 + 35%	413,350
$415,050	----------	$120,529.75 + 39.6%	$415,050

Married Filing Jointly of Qualifying Wiodw(er) – Schedule Y-1			
If Taxable Income Is: Over—	**But Not Over—**	**The Tax Is:**	**Of the Amount Over—**
$0	$18,550	$0 + 10%	$0
18,550	75,300	1,855.00 + 15%	18,550
75,300	151,900	10,367.50 + 25%	75,300
151,900	231,450	29,517.50 + 28%	151,900
231,450	413,350	51,791.50 + 33%	231,450
413,350	$466,950	111,818.50 + 35%	413,350
$466,950	----------	$130,578.50 + 39.6%	$466,950

Exhibit 25: Tax-Rate Schedules (2016 and 2017) (continued)

| Married Filing Separately – Schedule Y-2 | | | |
If Taxable Income Is: Over—	But Not Over—	The Tax Is:	Of the Amount Over—
$0	$9,275	$0 + 10%	$0
9,275	37,650	927.50 + 15%	9,275
37,650	75,950	5,183.75 + 25%	37,650
75,950	115,725	14,758.75 + 28%	75,950
115,725	206,675	25,895.75 + 33%	115,725
206,675	$233,475	55,909.25 + 35%	206,675
$233,475	----------	$65,289.25 + 39.6%	$233,475

| Head of Household – Schedule Z | | | |
If Taxable Income Is: Over—	But Not Over—	The Tax Is:	Of the Amount Over—
$0	$13,250	$0 + 10%	$0
13,250	50,400	1,325.00 + 15%	13,250
50,400	130,150	6,897.50 + 25%	50,400
130,150	210,800	26,835.00 + 28%	130,150
210,800	413,350	49,417.00+ 33%	210,800
413,350	$441,000	116,258.50 + 35%	413,350
$441, 000	----------	$125,936.00 + 39.6%	$441,000

Exhibit 25: Tax-Rate Schedules (2016 and 2017) (continued)

2017 TAX RATES AND BRACKETS

Single – Schedule X			
If Taxable Income Is: Over—	**But Not Over—**	**The Tax Is:**	**Of the Amount Over—**
$0	$9,325	$0 + 10%	$0
9,325	37,950	932.50 + 15%	9,325
37,950	91,900	5,226.25+ 25%	37,950
91,900	191,650	18,713.75 + 28%	91,900
191,650	416,700	46,643.75 + 33%	191,650
416,700	$418,400	120,910.25 + 35%	416,700
$418,400	----------	$121,505.25 + 39.6%	$418,400

Married Filing Jointly of Qualifying Wiodw(er) – Schedule Y-1			
If Taxable Income Is: Over—	**But Not Over—**	**The Tax Is:**	**Of the Amount Over—**
$0	$18,650	$0 + 10%	$0
18,650	75,900	1,865.00 + 15%	18,650
75,900	153,100	10,452.50 + 25%	75,900
153,100	233,350	29,752.50 + 28%	153,100
233,350	416,700	52,222.50 + 33%	233,350
416,700	$470,700	112,728.00+ 35%	416,700
$470,700	----------	$131,628.00 + 39.6%	$470,700

Exhibit 25: Tax-Rate Schedules (2016 and 2017) (continued)

Married Filing Separately – Schedule Y-2

If Taxable Income Is: Over—	But Not Over—	The Tax Is:	Of the Amount Over—
$0	$9,325	$0 + 10%	$0
9,325	37,950	932.50 + 15%	9,325
37,950	76,550	5,226.25 + 25%	37,950
76,550	116,675	14,876.25 + 28%	76,550
116,675	208,350	26,111.25 + 33%	116,675
208,350	$235,350	56,364.00 + 35%	208,350
$235,350	----------	$65,814.00 + 39.6%	$235,350

Head of Household – Schedule Z

If Taxable Income Is: Over—	But Not Over—	The Tax Is:	Of the Amount Over—
$0	$13,350	$0 + 10%	$0
13,350	50,800	1,335.00 + 15%	13,350
50,800	131,200	6,952.50 + 25%	50,800
131,200	212,500	27,052.50 + 28%	131,200
212,500	416,700	49,816.50 + 33%	212,500
416,700	$444,550	117,202.50+ 35%	416,700
$444,550	----------	$126,950.00 + 39.6%	$444,550

Exhibit 26: Standard Deduction Amount and Additional Deduction

Standard Deduction		
Filing Status	2016	2017
Single	$6,300	$6,350
Married, filing jointly/SS*	$12,600	$12,700
Head of household	$9,300	$9,350
Married, filing separately	$6,300	$6,350

*SS—Surviving spouse

Additional Standard Deduction*		
Filing Status	2016	2017
Single	$1,550	$1,550
Married, filing jointly/SS	$1,250	$1,250
Head of household	$1,550	$1,550
Married, filing separately	$1,250	$1,250

*Aged 65 and older or blind

Standard deduction for an individual claimed as a dependent by another taxpayer may not exceed the regular standard deduction and is limited to the greater of $1,050 in 2016 and 2017 or the sum of $350 (2016 and 2017) plus the individual's earned income.

Exhibit 27: Tax Formula for Individuals

Income (broadly conceived)	$xx,xxx
Less: Exclusions from Gross Income	(x,xxx)
Gross Income	$xx,xxx
Less: Deductions for Adjusted Gross Income	(x,xxx)
Adjusted Gross Income (AGI)	$xx,xxx
Less: The Greater of:	
Total Itemized Deductions or Standard Deduction	(x,xxx)
Less: Personal and Dependency Exemptions	(x,xxx)
Taxable Income	$xx,xxx

Exhibit 28: Dependency Exemption

Overview of the Rules for Claiming an Exemption for a Dependent

Caution. This table is only an overview of the rules. For details, see IRS Publication 17.

- You cannot claim any dependents if you, or your spouse if filing jointly, could be claimed as a dependent by another taxpayer.

- You cannot claim a married person who files a joint return as a dependent unless that joint return is only a claim for refund and there would be no tax liability for either spouse on separate returns.

- You cannot claim a person as a dependent unless that person is a U.S. citizen, U.S. resident alien, U.S. national, or a resident of Canada or Mexico, for some part of the year.[1]

- You cannot claim a person as a dependent unless that person is your **qualifying child** or **qualifying relative.**

Tests To Be a Qualifying Child	Tests To Be a Qualifying Relative
1. The child must be your son, daughter, stepchild, foster child, brother, sister, half brother, half sister, stepbrother, stepsister, or a descendant of any of them.	1. The person cannot be your qualifying child or the qualifying child of any other taxpayer.
2. The child must be (a) under age 19 at the end of the year, (b) under age 24 at the end of the year and a full-time student, or (c) any age if permanently and totally disabled.	2. The person either (a) must be related to you in one of the ways listed under *Relatives who do not have to live with you,* or (b) must live with you all year as a member of your household[2] (and your relationship must not violate local law).
3. The child must have lived with you for more than half of the year.[2]	3. The person's gross income for the year must be less than $4,000.[3]
4. The child must not have provided more than half of his or her own support for the year.	4. You must provide more than half of the person's total support for the year.[4]
5. If the child meets the rules to be a qualifying child of more than one person, you must be the person entitled to claim the child as a qualifying child.	

[1]There is an exception for certain adopted children.
[2]There are exceptions for temporary absences, children who were born or died during the year, children of divorced or separated parents, and kidnapped children.
[3]There is an exception if the person is disabled and has income from a sheltered workshop.
[4]There are exceptions for multiple support agreements, children of divorced or separated parents, and kidnapped children.

IRS Publication 17

NOTE: TO BE A QUALIFYING RELATIVE, THE INDIVIDUAL'S GROSS INCOME FOR THE YEAR MUST BE LESS THAN $4,050 (2016 and 2017). ANY INCOME RECEIVED BY THE INDIVIDUAL THAT IS EXCLUDED FROM INCOME (SUCH AS SOCIAL SECURITY BENEFITS) ARE ALSO CONSIDERED TOWARD SATISFYING THE SUPPORT GROSS INCOME THRESHOLD IF THE INDIVIDUAL USED THIS INCOME FOR THEIR OWN SUPPORT.

Exhibit 29: Deductible Travel Expenses

Expense	Description
Transportation	The cost of travel by airplane, train, or bus between your home and your business destination. If you were provided with a ticket or if you are riding free as the result of a frequent traveler or similar program, your cost is zero.
Taxi, Commuter Bus, and Limousine	Fares for these and other types of transportation between the airport or station and your hotel, or between the hotel and your work location away from home.
Baggage and Shipping	The cost of sending baggage and sample or display material between your regular and temporary work location.
Car	The costs of operating and maintaining your car when traveling away from home or business. You may deduct actual expenses or the standard mileage rate, including business-related tolls and parking. If you lease a car while away from home or business, you can deduct business-related expenses only.
Lodging	The cost of lodging if your business trip is overnight or long enough to require you to get substantial sleep or rest to properly perform your duties.
Meals	The cost of meals only if your business trip is overnight or long enough to require you to stop to get substantial sleep or rest. Includes amounts spent for food, beverages, taxes, and related tips. Only 50% of meal expenses are allowed as a deduction.
Cleaning	Cleaning and laundry expenses while away from home overnight.
Telephone	The cost of business calls while on your business trip, including business communication by fax machine or other communication devices.
Tips	Tips you pay for any expenses in this chart.
Other	Other similar ordinary and necessary expenses related to your business travel, such as public stenographer's fees and computer rental fees.

IRS Publication 334

Exhibit 30: Travel, Entertainment, Gift Expenses, and Reimbursements

Type of Reimbursement (or Other Expense Allowance) Arrangement	Employer Reports on Form W-2	Employee Shows on Form 2106
Accountable		
Actual expense reimbursement. Adequate accounting and excess returned.	Not reported.	Not shown if expenses do not exceed reimbursement.
Actual expense reimbursement. Adequate accounting and return of excess both required but excess not returned.	Excess reported as wages in box 1. Amount adequately accounted for is reported only in box 13—it is not reported in box 1.	All expenses (and reimbursements reported on Form W-2, box 13) only if some or all of the excess expenses are claimed. Otherwise, the form is not filed.
Per diem or mileage allowance (up to federal rate). Adequate accounting and excess returned.	Not reported.	All expenses and reimbursements only if excess expenses are claimed. Otherwise, form is not filed.
Per diem or mileage allowance (exceeds federal rate). Adequate accounting up to the federal rate only and excess not returned.	Excess reported as wages in box 1. Amount up to the federal rate is reported only in box 13—it is not reported in box 1.	All expenses (and reimbursements equal to the federal rate) only if expenses in excess of the federal rate are claimed. Otherwise, form is not filed.
Non-accountable		
Either adequate accounting or return of excess, or both, not required by plan.	Entire amount is reported as wages in box 1.	All expenses.
No Reimbursement		
	Normal reporting of wages, etc.	All expenses.

Exhibit 31: Child and Dependent Care Credit (2016 and 2017)

Adjusted Gross Income	Credit Rate	Maximum Credit	
		One Child	Two or More Children
$10,000 or less	30	720	1,440
10,001 – 12,000	29	696	1,392
12,001 – 14,000	28	672	1,344
14,001 – 16,000	27	648	1,296
16,001 – 18,000	26	624	1,248
18,001 – 20,000	25	600	1,200
20,001 – 22,000	24	576	1,152
22,001 – 24,000	23	552	1,104
24,001 – 26,000	22	528	1,056
26,001 – 28,000	21	504	1,008
28,001 and over	20	480	960

Exhibit 32: Section 79 Costs for Group Term Insurance

Age	Cost
Under 25	$0.05
25 through 29	$0.06
30 through 34	$0.08
35 through 39	$0.09
40 through 44	$0.10
45 through 49	$0.15
50 through 54	$0.23
55 through 59	$0.43
60 through 64	$0.66
65 through 69	$1.27
70 or older	$2.06

Exhibit 33: Section 179 Maximum Writeoffs

Tax Year Beginning In	Maximum Section 179
2016	$500,000
2017	$510,000

Exhibit 34: Retirement Plans

Qualified plans[A]		Other tax-advantaged plans	Nonqualified plans
Pension plans[B]	Profit-sharing plans[C]		
■ Defined benefit pension plans[D]	■ Profit-sharing plans (traditional)	■ SEP plans	■ Section 457 plans
■ Cash balance pension plans	■ Stock bonus plans	■ SARSEP plans	■ Nonqualified deferred compensation plans
■ Target benefit pension plans[D]	■ ESOPs	■ Traditional IRAs	■ Nonqualified stock option plans
■ Money purchase pension plans	■ Section 401(k) plans[E]	■ Roth IRAs	■ Incentive stock option plans
■ DB(k) plans	■ Thrift plans	■ SIMPLE IRAs	■ Phantom stock plans
	■ SIMPLE 401(k)	■ Section 403(b) plans	■ Restricted stock
	■ Age-based profit-sharing plans[D]		■ Employee stock purchase plans (ESPP)
	■ New comparability plans[D]		■ Junior class shares
			■ Stock appreciation rights (SARs)

[A] Distributions from qualified plans may qualify for 10-year forward averaging and other tax advantages; other plans and nonqualified plans do not

[B] Pension plans promise either a benefit or contributions; therefore, annual funding is mandatory

[C] Profit-sharing plans do not require mandatory annual funding

[D] These plans are tested for discrimination on the basis of benefits as opposed to contributions

[E] These plans are tested for discrimination regarding employee elective deferrals and employer-matching contributions

Exhibit 35: Comparison of Defined Benefit, Defined Contribution, and Cash Balance Plans

	Typical Defined Benefit Pension Plan (DB)	Typical Defined Contribution Plan (DC)	Cash Balance Pension Plan (CB)
Contribution	Actuarially determined	Percentage of salary (could be age weighted)	Percentage of salary (actuarially determined)
Investment Risk	Employer	Employee	Employer
Size of Work Force	Any size	Any size	Large
Investment Earnings	Employer responsible	Variable	Guaranteed
Social Security Integration	Yes	Yes*	Yes
Pension Benefit Guarantee Corporation Insurance	Yes	No	Yes
Section 401(k) Feature	DB(k)	Available in profit-sharing plan	No
Favors Older Entrants	Yes	No	No
Administrative Cost	Generally higher than DC Plans due to actuary and insurance	Generally lower than DB Plans	Generally higher than DC Plans due to actuary and insurance

*ESOPs are not eligible for integration.

Exhibit 36: ACP/ADP General Rules (Simplified)

If ADP for NHC:	Maximum ADP for HC is:
$\leq 2\%$	2 × ADP of NHC
$\geq 2\%$, but $\leq 8\%$	2% + ADP of NHC
$> 8\%$	1.25 × ADP of NHC

NHC = Non-highly compensated
HC = Highly compensated

Exhibit 37: Age-Based Profit-sharing Plan Illustration

Assume that a business owner is age 49, earns $230,000 per year, and elects to make a maximum contribution to a discretionary age-based profit-sharing plan. The plan will also benefit one employee, age 25, earning $18,000 per year.

	Business Owner	Employee	Total
Age	49	25	
Compensation	$230,000	$18,000	$248,000
Adjustment factor	0.294139	0.038265	
Age-adjusted compensation	$67,652	$689	$68,341
Allocation	$49,041	$499	$49,540
Annual allocation limit (100% or $54,000)	$54,000	$18,000	
Top-heavy minimum (3% of Compensation)	$0	$540	
Actual allocation	$49,041	$499	$49,540
Contribution rate	21%	3%	
Percent of contribution	98.90%	1.10%	

Although the maximum deductible limit for a profit-sharing plan is 25% of eligible compensation (25% × $248,000 = $62,000) the employer would only fund the plan so that he reached the $53,000 limit in 2016 and $54,000 in 2017.

$$\frac{\$67,652}{\$68,341} \times \$49,540 = \$49,041$$

$$\frac{\$689}{\$68,341} \times \$49,540 = \$499$$

Exhibit 38: Fringe Benefits by Entity Type

Benefit	Proprietorship	Partnership	S Corp	LLC	C Corp
Qualified plan	Yes	Yes	Yes	Yes	Yes
Group life	No	No	No	No	Yes
Group health*	Yes	Yes	Yes	Yes	Yes
Group disability	No	No	No	No	Yes
Medical reimbursement plans	No	No	No	No	Yes
Accidental death	No	No	No	No	Yes
Disability income plan	No	No	No	No	Yes
Employee death benefit					
–Employer provided	No	No	No	No	Yes
–Qualified plan	Yes	Yes	Yes	Yes	Yes
Cafeteria plan	No	No	No	No	Yes
Deferred compensation	No	No	No	No	Yes

LLC = Limited Liability Company
*Self-employed taxpayers and wage earners who are more than 2% shareholders of an S corporation can take a 100% deduction (not to exceed net earnings from self-employment) for amounts paid for health insurance for taxpayers, spouses, and dependents.

Exhibit 39: Keogh (Self-Employed) Worksheet for a Single Profit-Sharing Plan or a Single Money Purchase Pension Plan in 2017

Line 1	Net business profits (from Schedule C)	$100,000
Line 2	Deduction for self-employment tax (From IRS Form 1040) (given)	$7,065
Line 3	Adjusted net business profits (subtract Line 2 from line 1)	$92,935
Line 4	Contribution percentage	0.25
Line 5	Contribution factor (add 1.00 to line 4)	1.25
Line 6	Adjusted earned income (divide line 3 by line 5)	$74,348
Line 7	Maximum earned income on which contributions can be based (enter $270,000*)	$270,000
Line 8	Final earned income (the lesser of line 6 and line 7)	$74,348
Line 9	Preliminary contribution amount (multiply line 4 by line 8, round down to closest dollar)	$18,587
Line 10	Maximum dollar contribution amount (enter $54,000*)	$54,000
Line 11	Contribution amount (the lesser of line 9 and line 10)	$18,587

*Maximum limits for 2017.

Exhibit 40: IRA Current Phaseout Limits

Traditional IRAs

	Taxpayer Filing Status	
Tax Year	Phaseout Range Single	Phaseout Range Married Filing Jointly
2016	$61,000–$71,000	$98,000–$118,000
2017	$62,000–$72,000	$99,000–$119,000

An individual is not considered an active participant in an employer-sponsored retirement plan solely because his spouse is an active participant. However, when only one spouse is an active participant, the nonparticipant spouse will have his deduction phased out at AGI levels between $184,000 and $194,000 in 2016 and $186,000 and $196,000 in 2017.

ROTH IRAs

Taxpayer Filing Status			
Modified AGI Phaseout Ranges			
Tax Year	Single	Married Filing Jointly	Married Filing Separately
2016	$117,000–$132,000	$184,000–$194,000	$0–$10,000
2017	$118,000–$133,000	$186,000–$196,000	$0–$10,000

Exhibit 41: Table V—Ordinary Life Annuities
One Life—Expected Return Multiples
(Reg. Section 1.72-9)

Age	Multiple	Age	Multiple	Age	Multiple
5	77.7	42	41.7	79	10.8
6	76.7	43	40.7	80	10.2
7	75.8	44	39.8	81	9.7
8	74.8	45	38.8	82	9.1
9	73.8	46	37.9	83	8.6
10	72.8	47	37.0	84	8.1
11	71.8	48	36.0	85	7.6
12	70.8	49	35.1	86	7.1
13	69.9	50	34.2	87	6.7
14	68.9	51	33.3	88	6.3
15	67.9	52	32.3	89	5.9
16	66.9	53	31.4	90	5.5
17	66.0	54	30.5	91	5.2
18	65.0	55	29.6	92	4.9
19	64.0	56	28.7	93	4.6
20	63.0	57	27.9	94	4.3
21	62.1	58	27.0	95	4.1
22	61.1	59	26.1	96	3.8
23	60.1	60	25.2	97	3.6
24	59.1	61	24.4	98	3.4
25	58.2	62	23.5	99	3.1
26	57.2	63	22.7	100	2.9
27	56.2	64	21.8	101	2.7
28	55.3	65	21.0	102	2.5
29	54.3	66	20.2	103	2.3
30	53.3	67	19.4	104	2.1
31	52.4	68	18.6	105	1.9
32	51.4	69	17.8	106	1.7
33	50.4	70	17.0	107	1.5
34	49.4	71	16.3	108	1.4
35	48.5	72	15.5	109	1.2
36	47.5	73	14.8	110	1.1
37	46.5	74	14.1	111	0.9
38	45.6	75	13.4	112	0.8
39	44.6	76	12.7	113	0.7
40	43.6	77	12.1	114	0.6
41	42.7	78	11.4	115	0.5

Exhibit 42: Table VI—Ordinary Joint Life and Last Survivor Annuities Two Lives—Expected Return Multiples (Reg. Section 1.72-9)

Ages	65	66	67	68	69	70	71	72	73	74
65	26.2	25.8	25.4	25.0	24.6	24.3	23.9	23.7	23.4	23.1
66	25.8	25.3	24.9	24.5	24.1	23.7	23.4	23.1	22.8	22.5
67	25.4	24.9	24.4	24.0	23.6	23.2	22.8	22.5	22.2	21.9
68	25.0	24.5	24.0	23.5	23.1	22.7	22.3	22.0	21.6	21.3
69	24.6	24.1	23.6	23.1	22.6	22.2	21.8	21.4	21.1	20.8
70	24.3	23.7	23.2	22.7	22.2	21.8	21.3	20.9	20.6	20.2
71	23.9	23.4	22.8	22.3	21.8	21.3	20.9	20.5	20.1	19.7
72	23.7	23.1	22.5	22.0	21.4	20.9	20.5	20.0	19.6	19.3
73	23.4	22.8	22.2	21.6	21.1	20.6	20.1	19.6	19.2	18.8
74	23.1	22.5	21.9	21.3	20.8	20.2	19.7	19.3	18.8	18.4
75	22.9	22.3	21.6	21.0	20.5	19.9	19.4	18.9	18.4	18.0
76	22.7	22.0	21.4	20.8	20.2	19.6	19.1	18.6	18.1	17.6
77	22.5	21.8	21.2	20.6	19.9	19.4	18.8	18.3	17.8	17.3
78	22.4	21.7	21.0	20.3	19.7	19.1	18.5	18.0	17.5	17.0
79	22.2	21.5	20.8	20.1	19.5	18.9	18.3	17.7	17.2	16.7
80	22.1	21.3	20.6	20.0	19.3	18.7	18.1	17.5	16.9	16.4
81	21.9	21.2	20.5	19.8	19.1	18.5	17.9	17.3	16.7	16.2
82	21.8	21.1	20.4	19.7	19.0	18.3	17.7	17.1	16.5	15.9
83	21.7	21.0	20.2	19.5	18.8	18.2	17.5	16.9	16.3	15.7
84	21.6	20.9	20.1	19.4	18.7	18.0	17.4	16.7	16.1	15.5
85	21.6	20.8	20.1	19.3	18.6	17.9	17.3	16.6	16.0	15.4
86	21.5	20.7	20.0	19.2	18.5	17.8	17.1	16.5	15.8	15.2
87	21.4	20.7	19.9	19.2	18.4	17.7	17.0	16.4	15.7	15.1
88	21.4	20.6	19.8	19.1	18.3	17.6	16.9	16.3	15.6	15.0
89	21.3	20.5	19.8	19.0	18.3	17.6	16.9	16.2	15.5	14.9
90	21.3	20.5	19.7	19.0	18.2	17.5	16.8	16.1	15.4	14.8
91	21.3	20.5	19.7	18.9	18.2	17.4	16.7	16.0	15.4	14.7
92	21.2	20.4	19.6	18.9	18.1	17.4	16.7	16.0	15.3	14.6
93	21.2	20.4	19.6	18.8	18.1	17.3	16.6	15.9	15.2	14.6
94	21.2	20.4	19.6	18.8	18.0	17.3	16.6	15.9	15.2	14.5
95	21.1	20.3	19.6	18.8	18.0	17.3	16.5	15.8	15.1	14.5
96	21.1	20.3	19.5	18.8	18.0	17.2	16.5	15.8	15.1	14.4
97	21.1	20.3	19.5	18.7	18.0	17.2	16.5	15.8	15.1	14.4
98	21.1	20.3	19.5	18.7	17.9	17.2	16.4	15.7	15.0	14.3
99	21.1	20.3	19.5	18.7	17.9	17.2	16.4	15.7	15.0	14.3

Exhibit 42: Table VI—Ordinary Joint Life and Last Survivor Annuities Two Lives—Expected Return Multiples (Reg. Section 1.72-9) (continued)

Ages	65	66	67	68	69	70	71	72	73	74
100	21.1	20.3	19.5	18.7	17.9	17.1	16.4	15.7	15.0	14.3
101	21.1	20.2	19.4	18.7	17.9	17.1	16.4	15.6	14.9	14.2
102	21.1	20.2	19.4	18.6	17.9	17.1	16.4	15.6	14.9	14.2
103	21.0	20.2	19.4	18.6	17.9	17.1	16.3	15.6	14.9	14.2
104	21.0	20.2	19.4	18.6	17.8	17.1	16.3	15.6	14.9	14.2
105	21.0	20.2	19.4	18.6	17.8	17.1	16.3	15.6	14.9	14.2
106	21.0	20.2	19.4	18.6	17.8	17.1	16.3	15.6	14.8	14.1
107	21.0	20.2	19.4	18.6	17.8	17.0	16.3	15.6	14.8	14.1
108	21.0	20.2	19.4	18.6	17.8	17.0	16.3	15.5	14.8	14.1
109	21.0	20.2	19.4	18.6	17.8	17.0	16.3	15.5	14.8	14.1
110	21.0	20.2	19.4	18.6	17.8	17.0	16.3	15.5	14.8	14.1
111	21.0	20.2	19.4	18.6	17.8	17.0	16.3	15.5	14.8	14.1
112	21.0	20.2	19.4	18.6	17.8	17.0	16.3	15.5	14.8	14.1
113	21.0	20.2	19.4	18.6	17.8	17.0	16.3	15.5	14.8	14.1
114	21.0	20.2	19.4	18.6	17.8	17.0	16.3	15.5	14.8	14.1
115	21.0	20.2	19.4	18.6	17.8	17.0	16.3	15.5	14.8	14.1

Exhibit 43: Indexed Limits for Pension and Other Plans

Type of Limit	2016	2017
Defined benefit plan maximum benefit limit	$210,000	$215,000
Defined contribution plan maximum limit	$53,000	$54,000
Section 401(k) plan elective deferral limit (under age 50)	$18,000	$18,000
IRA limit	$5,500	$5,500
Catch-up provision		
Section 401(k)/SARSEP/Section 457/Section 403(b) plans	$6,000	$6,000
SIMPLE	$3,000	$3,000
IRA catch-up	$1,000	$1,000
HC employee—Section 414(q)		
Greater than 5% owner	Any	Any
Compensation	$120,000	$120,000
Key employee		
Officer Section 416(i)	$170,000	$175,000
Greater than 1% owner	$150,000	$150,000
Greater than 5% owner	Any	Any
SIMPLE deferral	$12,500	$12,500
SEP plan		
Minimum earnings	$600	$600
Maximum earnings	$265,000	$270,000
Section 457 plan	$18,000	$18,000
Maximum covered compensation	$265,000	$270,000
Social Security integration		
Taxable wage base (TWB)	$118,500	$127,200
Medicare		
Wage base	Unlimited	Unlimited
PBGC maximum monthly benefit (up to the annually indexed limit)	$5,011	$5,369

Exhibit 44: Table III—Uniform Lifetime, IRS Publication 590*

Age	Applicable Divisor	Age	Applicable Divisor
70	27.4	93	9.6
71	26.5	94	9.1
72	25.6	95	8.6
73	24.7	96	8.1
74	23.8	97	7.6
75	22.9	98	7.1
76	22.0	99	6.7
77	21.2	100	6.3
78	20.3	101	5.9
79	19.5	102	5.5
80	18.7	103	5.2
81	17.9	104	4.9
82	17.1	105	4.5
83	16.3	106	4.2
84	15.5	107	3.9
85	14.8	108	3.7
86	14.1	109	3.4
87	13.4	110	3.1
88	12.7	111	2.9
89	12.0	112	2.6
90	11.4	113	2.4
91	10.8	114	2.1
92	10.2	115	1.9

*Use this table if the beneficiary is someone other than a spouse who is more than 10 years younger than the beneficiary.

Exhibit 45: Self-Employed Person's Rate Table

Column A	Column B
If the plan contribution rate is: (shown as a percentage)	The self-employed person's rate is: (shown as a decimal)
1	0.009901
2	0.019608
3	0.029126
4	0.038462
5	0.047619
6	0.056604
7	0.065421
8	0.074074
9	0.082569
10	0.090909
11	0.099099
12	0.107143
13	0.115044
14	0.122807
15	0.130435
16	0.137931
17	0.145299
18	0.152542
19	0.159664
20	0.166667
21	0.173554
22	0.180328
23	0.186992
24	0.193548
25*	0.200000*

*The deduction for annual employer contributions to a SEP cannot exceed 25% of the common-law employee participant's compensation or 20% of the self-employed compensation (figured without deducting contributions) from the business that has the plan. The factor is calculated as follows: 0.25 ÷ 1.25 = 0.20

Note: The deduction for annual employer contributions to a profit-sharing or money purchase plan is also limited to 25% of the employee's compensation, or 20% of the self-employed compensation.

Exhibit 46: Summary of Retirement Plans

	Defined benefit pension plan	Money purchase pension plan	Profit-sharing plan	Stock bonus plan	Savings or thrift plan	Section 401(k) plan	ESOP	SEP/ SARSEP plan	Cash balance pension plan	Target benefit pension plan	SIMPLE
Employer contributions											
Mandatory	✓	✓							✓	✓	✓
Discretionary			✓	✓	✓	✓	✓	✓			✓
Employee contributions											
Pretax	DB(k)		✓			✓		✓ (SARSEP only)			✓
After tax		✓	✓		✓ (Usually)	✓					
Investment in employer stock											
Restricted	✓	✓						✓	✓	✓	
Not restricted			✓	✓	✓	✓	✓				
Guaranteed investment return									✓		
Right to vote	N/A	N/A	No	Yes	No	N/A	On some matters	N/A	N/A	N/A	N/A
Leverage borrowing to purchase company stock	N/A	N/A	N/A	N/A	N/A	N/A	✓	N/A	N/A	N/A	N/A
In-service withdrawals, timing and form of distribution before retirement	Age 62 or older	Age 62 or older	Yes	Yes	Yes	Yes	Yes	Yes	No	No	Yes
At retirement: In cash	✓	✓	✓	Perhaps	✓	✓	Perhaps	✓	Possible	Possible	✓
Plan investment in employer securities limit	10%	10%	Unlimited	Unlimited	Unlimited	Unlimited	Unlimited	N/A	10%	10%	N/A
Integration	Yes	Yes	Yes	Yes	Yes	Yes*	No	Yes/No	Yes	Yes	No
Forfeitures reduce plan costs	Must	Can	Can	Can	Can	Can	Can	N/A	Must	Can	N/A
10-year forward averaging	Yes	Yes	Yes	Yes	Yes	Yes	Yes	No	Yes	Yes	Section 401(k)
Investment risk											
Employee		✓	✓	✓	✓	✓	✓	✓		✓	✓
Employer	✓								✓		

* Only the profit-sharing portion of a Section 401(k) plan can be integrated.

Summary of Plans (*continued*)

	Defined benefit pension plan	Money purchase pension plan	Profit-sharing plan	Stock bonus plan	Savings or thrift plan	Section 401(k) plan	ESOP	SEP/ SARSEP plan	Cash balance pension plan	Target benefit pension plan	SIMPLE
PBGC insurance	Yes	No	No	No	No	No	No	No	Yes	No	No
Actuarial costs	Yes	No	No	No	No	No	No	No	Yes	Yes	No
Vesting											
Immediate (100%)	No	No	No	No	No	No	No	Yes	No	No	Yes
5-year cliff or 3–7 graduated	Yes	No	No	No	No	No	No	No	Yes	No	No
3-year cliff or 2–6 graduated	Top-heavy	Yes	Yes	Yes	Yes	Yes	Yes	No	3-year cliff only	Yes	No
Favors older (O) or younger (Y) employees	O	Y	Y	Y	Y	Y	Y	Y	Y	O	Y

Exhibit 47: Determining Full Retirement Age

Full Retirement Age for Retired Worker and Spouse Benefits	Year of Birth	Full Retirement Age for Surviving Spouse Benefits
	Before 1938	65
65 and 2 months	1938	65
65 and 4 months	1939	65
65 and 6 months	1940	65 and 2 months
65 and 8 months	1941	65 and 4 months
65 and 10 months	1942	65 and 6 months
66	1943	65 and 8 months
66	1944	65 and 10 months
66	1945–54	66
66 and 2 months	1955	66
66 and 4 months	1956	66
66 and 6 months	1957	66 and 2 months
66 and 8 months	1958	66 and 4 months
66 and 10 months	1959	66 and 6 months
67	1960	66 and 8 months
67	1961	66 and 10 months
67	1962 and after	67

Exhibit 48: Reduced Retirement Benefits for Workers

| Year of Birth | You will receive this percentage of your PIA if you retire at age: | | | | |
	62	63	64	65	66
Before 1938	80.0%	86.6%	93.3%	100.0%	—
1938	79.1%	85.5%	92.2%	98.8%	—
1939	78.3%	84.4%	91.1%	97.7%	—
1940	77.5%	83.3%	90.0%	96.6%	—
1941	76.6%	82.2%	88.8%	95.5%	—
1942	75.8%	81.1%	87.7%	94.4%	—
1943–1954	75.0%	80.0%	86.6%	93.3%	100.0%
1955	74.1%	79.1%	85.5%	92.2%	98.8%
1956	73.3%	78.3%	84.4%	91.1%	97.7%
1957	72.5%	77.5%	83.3%	90.0%	96.6%
1958	71.6%	76.6%	82.2%	88.8%	95.5%
1959	70.8%	75.8%	81.1%	87.7%	94.4%
1960 and later	70.0%	75.0%	80.0%	86.6%	93.3%

Note: Decimals are rounded down.

You may retire at ages between the ones shown. The reduction factor applied to the PIA is 5/9 of 1% for each of the first 36 months that entitlement is before the FRA, plus 5/12 of 1% for each such month in excess of 36. These reduction factors are for workers only. Different reduction factors are used for spouses.

Exhibit 49: Assets Passing Through and Around the Probate Process

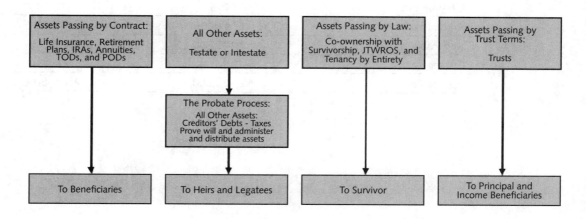

Exhibit 50: Unified Tax Rate Schedule (for Gift and Estate Tax)

Over $0 but not over $10,000	18% of such amount
Over $10,000 but not over $20,000	$1,800 plus 20% of the excess of such amount over $10,000
Over $20,000 but not over $40,000	$3,800 plus 22% of the excess of such amount over $20,000
Over $40,000 but not over $60,000	$8,200 plus 24% of the excess of such amount over $40,000
Over $60,000 but not over $80,000	$13,000 plus 26% of the excess of such amount over $60,000
Over $80,000 but not over $100,000	$18,200 plus 28% of the excess of such amount over $80,000
Over $100,000 but not over $150,000	$23,800 plus 30% of the excess of such amount over $100,000
Over $150,000 but not over $250,000	$38,800 plus 32% of the excess of such amount over $150,000
Over $250,000 but not over $500,000	$70,800 plus 34% of the excess of such amount over $250,000
Over $500,000 but not over $750,000	$155,800 plus 37% of the excess of such amount over $500,000
Over $750,000 but not over $1,000,000	$248,300 plus 39% of the excess of such amount over $750,000
Over $1 million	$345,800 plus 40% of the excess of such amount over $1,000,000

Lifetime gifts	2016	2017
Annual exclusion	$14,000	$14,000
Applicable credit	$2,125,800	$2,141,800
Estates		
Applicable credit	$2,125,800	$2,141,800

Exhibit 51: GSTT Rates and Exemptions

Year	GSTT Rate	GSTT Exemption
2016	40%	$5,450,000
2017	40%	$5,490,000

Exhibit 52: Gift Tax Formula

(1) Total gifts in current year (fair market value of all gifts) $ _____

(2) Less:

   (a) One-half of value of gifts split with spouse   _____

   (b) Annual exclusions ($14,000 per donee for present interests*)   _____

   (c) Marital deduction (can be unlimited if spouse is a US citizen)   _____

   (d) Charitable deduction (can be unlimited)   _____

   (e) Total subtractions   _____

(3) Equals: Taxable gifts in current year $ _____

(4) Add: Post-1976 taxable gifts made in previous years   _____

(5) Equals: Total taxable gifts to date (tax base)   _____

(6) Tentative tax on total taxable gifts to date   _____

(7) Less: Tax paid or deemed paid on prior taxable gifts   (_____)

(8) Equals: Gift tax on current year taxable gifts before applicable credit   _____

(9) Less: Applicable credit   (_____)

(10) Equals: Gift tax due on current year taxable gifts $ _____

*$14,000 in 2016 and 2017

Exhibit 53: Estate Tax Formula

(1) Total gross estate $ _____

(2) Less: Expenses, debts, and losses:

    (a) Funeral and administrative expenses   _____

    (b) Debts of decedent, mortgages, losses   _____

(3) Equals: Adjusted gross estate (AGE)*   _____

(4) Less: Total allowable deductions:

    (a) Charitable deduction   _____

    (b) Marital deduction   _____

    (c) State death taxes   _____

    Total allowable deductions   (_____)

(5) Equals: Taxable estate $ _____

(6) Add: Adjusted taxable gifts (post-1976)   _____

(7) Compute: Tentative tax base   _____

(8) Compute: Tentative tax   _____

(9) Less: Tax paid or deemed paid on prior taxable gifts   (_____)

(10) Equals: Estate tax before reduction for allowable credits   _____

(11) Less:

    Applicable credit amount   _____

    Other credits   _____

(12) Equals: Estate Tax Liability $ _____

*The term *adjusted gross estate* is not on Form 706; however, this concept applies to Section 6166. Section 303 and Section 2032A and may be tested on the exam.

Exhibit 54: Charitable Remainder Trusts

	CRAT	CRUT	Pooled Income Fund
Value of charitable gift	Total value of property—PV of retained interest income	Total value of property—PV of retained interest income	Total value of property—PV of retained interest income
Income recipient	Noncharitable beneficiary (usually donor)	Noncharitable beneficiary (usually donor)	Noncharitable beneficiary (usually donor)
Payment	At least 5% of initial FMV of assets paid at least annually for life or term ≤20 years (similar to fixed annuity); cannot exceed 50% of value of trust	At least 5% of current FMV of assets (revalued annually) paid at least annually for life or term ≤20 years (similar to variable annuity); cannot exceed 50% of value of trust	Trust rate of return for year
Remainderman	Charity	Charity	Charity
Additional contributions	No	Yes	Yes
When income Is insufficient for payout	Must invade corpus	Can pay up to income and make up deficiency in subsequent year	N/A
Can hold tax-exempt securities	Yes	Yes	No

Exhibit 55: Structure of a Trust

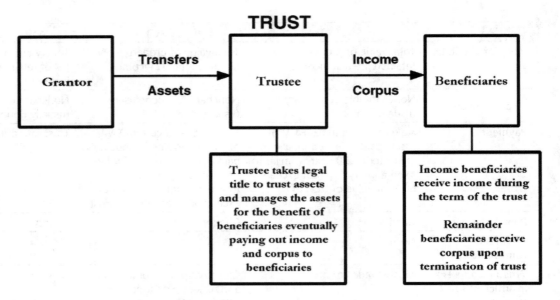

Exhibit 56: Parties to a Trust

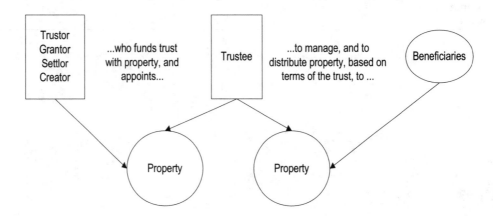

Reasons for creating trusts: 1. To provide for multiple beneficiaries.
2. To manage property if grantor becomes incapacitated.
3. To protect beneficiaries from themselves and others.
4. To avoid or reduce taxes.

Trust characteristics: 1. Revocable or irrevocable.
2. Intervivos or testamentary.
3. Funded or unfunded.

Exhibit 57: Estate Tax Reduction Techniques

1. Do not overqualify the estate. Use the applicable exclusion amount.

2. Do not underqualify the estate. Use the appropriate amount for the marital deduction, generally, to reduce the estate tax to zero.

3. Generally, remove life insurance from the estate of the client.

4. Change the ownership of life insurance or use irrevocable life insurance trust (must remove all incidents of ownership).

5. Use lifetime gifts. Make use of annual exclusions with gift splitting.

6. Use basic trusts.

7. Use charitable contributions, transfers, and trusts.

Exhibit 58: Common Estate Planning Mistakes

1. Invalid, Out-of-Date, or Poorly Drafted Will.

   - Will does not meet statutory requirements.

   - Will does not contemplate changes in tax laws.

   - Decedent has moved to another state of residence and domicile.

   - Will has no residuary clause or lacks drafting specificities.

2. Simple Wills (Sweetheart or I Love You Wills).

   - Leaving everything to a spouse may cause an overqualification of the estate.

   - Mismanagement of assets may occur.

3. Improperly Arranged or Inadequate Life Insurance.

   - Failure to remove proceeds from estate.

   - Leaving proceeds directly to beneficiary.

   - Inadequate life insurance coverage.

4. Possible Adverse Consequences of Jointly Held Property.

   - Joint title may result in state and federal gift and estate tax. If joint title results in a completed gift, consequences may be federal and state gift tax liability.

   - Double estate taxation. For jointly owned property (not by spouses), property value may be included in first decedent's estate and then included in survivor's estate (recall credit for tax on prior transfer).

- Property passed by law, not by will (JTWROS), can thwart the intentions of decedent because property will pass automatically by law.

- Jointly held property allows survivor to name ultimate remainderman. Decedent may not be able to direct property to person or entity wishes.

5. Estate Liquidity Problems.

   - Insufficient cash assets.

   - Inadequate planning.

6. Wrong Executor/Trustee/Manager.

   - Poor estate management always makes costs increase.

   - Potential conflicts of interest.

   - Proximity problems/family conflict.

   - Named executor/trustee is incapable of administering estate efficiently and effectively.

Exhibit 59: CFP Certification Examination Job Task Domains (page 1 of 5)

CERTIFIED FINANCIAL PLANNER
BOARD OF STANDARDS, INC.

CFP® Certification Examination
Job Task Domains

The following Job Task Domains are based on the results of CFP Board's 2009 Job Analysis Study and will serve as the blueprint for the March 2012 and later administrations of the CFP® Certification Examination. Each exam question will be linked to one of the following domains, in the approximate percentages indicated following the general headings.

Targeted First Test Administration: March 2012

8 Major Domains:

1. Establishing and Defining the Client-Planner Relationship (8%)

2. Gathering Information Necessary to Fulfill the Engagement (9%)

3. Analyzing and Evaluating the Client's Current Financial Status (25%)

4. Developing the Recommendation(s) (25%)

5. Communicating the Recommendation(s) (9%)

6. Implementing the Recommendation(s) (9%)

7. Monitoring the Recommendation(s) (5%)

8. Practicing within Professional and Regulatory Standards (10%)

Exhibit 59: CFP Certification Examination Job Task Domains
(page 2 of 5)

2

Domain 1 - Establishing and Defining the Client-Planner Relationship (8%)

A. Identify the client (e.g., individual, family, business, organization)
B. Discuss financial planning needs and expectations of the client
C. Discuss the financial planning process with the client
D. Explain scope of services offered by the CFP® professional and his/her firm
E. Assess and communicate the CFP® professional's ability to meet the client's needs and expectations
F. Identify and resolve apparent and potential conflicts of interest in client relationships
G. Discuss the client's responsibilities and those of the CFP® professional
H. Define and document the scope of the engagement with the client
I. Provide client disclosures
    1. Regulatory disclosure
    2. Compensation arrangements and associated potential conflicts of interest

Domain 2 - Gathering Information Necessary to Fulfill the Engagement (9%)

A. Identify the client's values and attitudes
    1. Explore with the client their personal and financial needs, priorities and goals
    2. Explore the client's time horizon for each goal
    3. Assess the client's level of knowledge and experience with financial matters
    4. Assess the client's risk exposures (e.g., longevity, economic, liability, healthcare)
    5. Assess the client's risk tolerances (e.g., investment, economic, liability, healthcare)
B. Gather Data
    1. Summary of assets (e.g., cost basis information, beneficiary designations and titling)
    2. Summary of liabilities (e.g., balances, terms, interest rates). Summary of abilities (e.g., balances, terms, interest rates)
    3. Summary of income and expenses
    4. Estate planning documents
    5. Education plan and resources
    6. Retirement plan information
    7. Employee benefits
    8. Government benefits (e.g., Social Security, Medicare)
    9. Special circumstances (e.g., legal documents and agreements, family situations)
    10. Tax documents
    11. Investment statements
    12. Insurance policies and documents (e.g., life, health, disability, liability)
    13. Closely held business documents (e.g., shareholder agreements)
    14. Inheritances, windfalls, and other large lump sums
C. Recognize need for additional information

Domain 3 - Analyzing and Evaluating the Client's Current Financial Status (25%)

A. Evaluate and document the strengths and vulnerabilities of the client's current financial situation
    1. Financial status
        A. Statement of financial position/balance sheet
        B. Cash flow statement

Exhibit 59: CFP Certification Examination Job Task Domains (page 3 of 5)

3

        C. Budget
        D. Capital needs analysis (e.g., insurance, retirement, major purchases)

2. Risk management and insurance evaluation
    A. Insurance coverage
    B. Retained risks
    C. Asset protection (e.g., titling, trusts, business form)
    D. Client liquidity (e.g., emergency fund)

3. Benefits evaluation
    A. Government benefits (e.g., Social Security, Medicare)
    B. Employee benefits

4. Investment evaluation
    A. Asset allocation
    B. Investment strategies
    C. Investment types

5. Tax evaluation
    A. Current, deferred and future tax liabilities
    B. Income types
    C. Special situations (e.g., stock options, international tax issues)

6. Retirement evaluation
    A. Retirement plans and strategies (e.g., pension options, annuitization)
    B. Accumulation planning
    C. Distribution planning

7. Estate planning evaluation
    A. Estate documents
    B. Estate tax liabilities
    C. Ownership of assets
    D. Beneficiary designations
    E. Gifting strategies

8. Business ownership
    A. Business form
    B. Employer benefits
    C. Succession planning and exit strategy
    D. Risk management

9. Education planning evaluation
    A. Sources of financing
    B. Tax considerations

10. Other considerations
    A. Special circumstances (e.g., divorce, disabilities, family dynamics)
    B. Inheritances, windfalls, and other large lump sums
    C. Charitable planning
    D. Eldercare (e.g., CCRCs, LTC, Nursing Home)

B. Identify and use appropriate tools and techniques to conduct analyses (e.g., financial calculators, financial planning software, simulators, research services)

Exhibit 59: CFP Certification Examination Job Task Domains (page 4 of 5)

4

Domain 4 - Developing the Recommendation(s) (25%)
    A. Synthesize findings from analysis of client's financial status
    B. Consider alternatives to meet the client's goals and objectives
        1. Conduct scenario analysis (e.g., changing lifestyle variables)
        2. Conduct sensitivity analysis (e.g., changing assumptions such as inflation rate, rates of return, time horizon)
    C. Consult with other professionals on technical issues outside of planner's expertise
    D. Develop recommendations
        1. Considering client attitudes, values and beliefs
        2. Considering behavioral finance issues (e.g., anchoring, overconfidence, recency)
        3. Consider interrelationships among financial planning recommendations
    E. Document recommendations

Domain 5 - Communicating the Recommendation(s) (9%)
    A. Present financial plan to the client and provide education
        1. Client goals review
        2. Assumptions
        3. Observations and findings
        4. Alternatives
        5. Recommendations
    B. Obtain feedback from the client and revise the recommendations as appropriate
    C. Provide documentation of plan recommendations and any applicable product disclosures to client
    D. Verify client acceptance of recommendations

Domain 6 - Implementing the Recommendation(s) (9%)
    A. Create a prioritized implementation plan with timeline
    B. Assign responsibilities (e.g., CFP® professional, client, other professional(s))
    C. Support the client directly or indirectly with implementation of the recommendation(s)
    D. Coordinate and share information, as authorized, with others
    E. Define monitoring responsibilities with the client (e.g., explain what will be monitored, frequency   of monitoring, communication method(s)

Domain 7 - Monitoring the Recommendation(s) (5%)
    A. Discuss and evaluate changes in the client's personal circumstances (e.g., aging issues, change in employment)
    B. Review the performance and progress of the plan with the client
    C. Review and evaluate changes in the legal, tax and economic environments
    D. Make recommendations to accommodate changed circumstances
    E. Review scope of work and redefine engagement as appropriate
    F. Provide client ongoing support (e.g., counseling, education)

Exhibit 59: CFP Certification Examination Job Task Domains (page 5 of 5)

5

Domain 8 - Practicing within Professional and Regulatory Standards (10%)
    A. Adhere to CFP Board's *Code of Ethics and Professional Responsibility* and *Rules of Conduct*
    B. Understand CFP Board's *Disciplinary Rules and Procedures*
    C. Work within CFP Board's *Financial Planning Practice Standards*
    D. Manage practice risk (e.g., documentation, monitor client noncompliance with recommendation(s)
    E. Maintain awareness of and comply with regulatory and legal guidelines

Exhibit 60: CFP Certification Examination Principal Topics (page 1 of 2)

CERTIFIED FINANCIAL PLANNER
BOARD OF STANDARDS, INC.

CFP® Certification Examination
Principal Topics

The following Principal Topics are based on the results of CFP Board's 2009 Job Analysis Study and serve as a curricular framework.

General Principles of Financial Planning
- Financial planning process
- Financial statements
- Cash flow management
- Financing strategies
- Function, purpose, and regulation of financial institutions
- Education planning
- Financial planning for special circumstances
- Economic concepts
- Time value of money concepts and calculations
- Financial services regulations and requirements
- Business law
- Consumer protection laws

Insurance Planning
- Principles of risk and insurance
- Analysis and evaluation of risk exposures
- Health insurance and health care cost management (individual)
- Disability income insurance (individual)
- Long-term care insurance (individual)
- Annuities
- Life insurance (individual)
- Income taxation of life insurance
- Business uses of insurance
- Insurance needs analysis
- Insurance policy and company selection

Investment Planning
- Characteristics, uses and taxation of investment vehicles
- Types of investment risk
- Quantitative investment concepts
- Measures of investment returns
- Asset allocation and portfolio diversification
- Bond and stock valuation concepts
- Portfolio development and analysis
- Investment strategies

Income Tax Planning
- Income tax law fundamentals
- Tax compliance
- Income tax fundamentals and calculations
- Characteristics and income taxation of business entities
- Income taxation of trusts and estates
- Basis
- Tax consequences of the disposition of property
- Alternative minimum tax (AMT)
- Tax reduction/management techniques
- Passive activity and at-risk rules
- Tax implications of special circumstances
- Charitable contributions and deductions

  CERTIFIED FINANCIAL PLANNER™   CFP®

Exhibit 60: CFP Certification Examination Principal Topics
(page 2 of 2)

2

Retirement Planning
- Retirement needs analysis
- Social Security (Old Age, Survivor, and Disability Insurance, OASDI)
- Types of retirement plans
- Qualified plan rules and options
- Other tax-advantaged retirement plans
- Regulatory considerations
- Key factors affecting plan selection for businesses
- Investment considerations for retirement plans
- Distribution rules, alternatives, and taxation

Estate Planning
- Characteristics and consequences of property titling
- Methods of property transfer at death
- Estate planning documents
- Gifting strategies
- Gift tax compliance and tax calculation
- Incapacity planning
- Estate tax compliance and tax calculation
- Sources for estate liquidity
- Powers of appointment
- Types, features, and taxation of trusts
- Qualified interest trusts
- Charitable transfers
- Use of life insurance in estate planning
- Marital deduction
- Intra-family and other business transfer techniques
- Deferral and minimization of estate taxes
- Generation-skipping transfer tax (GSTT)
- Fiduciaries
- Income in respect of a decedent (IRD)
- Postmortem estate planning techniques
- Estate planning for non-traditional relationships

Interpersonal Communication
- Client and planner attitudes, values, biases and behavioral characteristics and the impact on financial planning
- Principles of communication and counseling

Professional Conduct and Fiduciary Responsibility
- CFP Board's *Code of Ethics and Professional Responsibility* and *Rules of Conduct*
- CFP Board's *Financial Planning Practice Standards*
- CFP Board's *Disciplinary Rules and Procedures*

Exhibit 61: 2016 and 2017 Other Tax Limits

Child Tax Credit

	2016	2017
Maximum Credit	$1,000	$1,000
Refundability	15%	15%
Of Income	$3,000	$3,000

Adoption Credit

Maximum credit is $13,460 (2016) and $13,570 (2017) per eligible child.

Personal Exemption Phaseouts

Filing Status	2016	2017
Phaseout*	Begin Phaseout	Begin Phaseout
Married, filing jointly/SS	$311,300	$313,800
Head of household	$285,350	$287,650
Married, filing separately	$155,650	$156,900
Single	$259,400	$261,500

*2% for each $2,500 or fraction ($1,250 for married filing separately) above threshold.

Overall Limitation on Itemized Deduction

Filing Status	2016	2017
Overall Limitation on Itemized Deductions	AGI Limit	AGI Limit
Married Filing Jointly, Surviving Spouse	$311,300	$313,800
Head of Household	$285,350	$287,650
Married Filing Separately	$155,650	$156,900
Single	$259,400	$261,500

1. The reduction in itemized deductions is the lesser of 3% of the excess AGI or 80% of the itemized deductions otherwise allowable.

2. Certain itemized deductions are excluded from this reduction.

Kiddie Tax Threshold

2016	2017
$2,100	$2,100

Unearned income in excess of the threshold is taxed at the parents' rate.

A parent will be able to include a child's income on the parent's return if the child's income is more than $1,050 and less than $10,500 (2016 and 2017).

The exemption amount under Sections 55 and 59(j) for purposes of the alternative minimum tax is the lesser of (1) the sum of such child's earned income for the taxable year, plus $7,400 (2016) and $7,500 (2017), or (2) the AMT exemption amount for a single taxpayer.

Education Credits

Filing Status	2016 American Opportunity Tax Credit MAGI Phaseout	2017 American Opportunity Tax Credit MAGI Phaseout
Joint/Surviving Spouse	$160,000 – $180,000	$160,000 – $180,000
Single	$80,000 – $90,000	$80,000 – $90,000

For 2016 and 2017, the American Opportunity Tax Credit is 100% of the first $2,000 plus 25% of the next $2,000 of qualified higher education expenses.

Eligible Long-Term Care Premiums

Attained Age Before Year-End	2016	2017
40 or less	$390	$410
More than 40, but not more than 50	$730	$770
More than 50, but not more than 60	$1,460	$1,530
More than 60, but not more than 70	$3,900	$4,090
More than 70	$4,870	$5,110

Archer Medical Savings Accounts

	2016	2017
Self-Only Coverage		
Minimum required health plan deductible	$2,250	$2,250
Maximum allowable health plan deductible	$3,350	$3,350
Maximum allowed out-of-pocket limit	$4,450	$4,500
Family Coverage		
Minimum required health plan deductible	$4,450	$4,500
Maximum allowable health plan deductible	$6,700	$6,750
Maximum allowed out-of-pocket limit	$8,150	$8,250

Health Savings Accounts

	2016	2017
Self-Only Coverage		
Minimum required health plan deductible	≥$1,300	≥$1,300
Maximum allowed out-of-pocket limit	$6,550	$6,550
Contribution limit	$3,350	$3,400
Family Coverage		
Minimum required health plan deductible	≥$2,600	≥$2,600
Maximum allowed out-of-pocket limit	$13,100	$13,100
Contribution limit	$6,750	$6,750

Notes

Notes

Notes

Notes

Notes

Notes

Notes